FOREST HILLS

AN ILLUSTRATED HISTORY

FOREST HILLS

ROBERT MINTON

J. B. LIPPINCOTT COMPANY
PHILADELPHIA & NEW YORK

PICTURE CREDITS

Grateful acknowledgment is made to the following sources for pictures appearing as indicated:

Alex Webb: all color photos. David Levine: caricatures pp. 220–21. Jerome Scheurger: map p. 47.

Russ Adams: pp. 21, 110 top, 228–29. American Lawn Tennis (Courtesy of the Boston Public Library): p. 96. Bettman Archive: pp. 58 top, 102. *Boston Globe:* p. 224. Culver Pictures: pp. 44, 79, 80, 111 top. Mary Nolan Kelly: p. 206 top. George McGann: p. 219. New York Public Library: pp. 34, 36–37, 38, 50, 58 bottom left, 218. Tennis Hall of Fame (John Hoph): pp. 66–70. Underwood & Underwood: pp. 58 bottom right, 89, 90, 103, 111 bottom, 112, 114, 118, 125, 128, 129, 138, 143 left, 152 top, 153 bottom. UPI: pp. 192 left, 204, 205. USTA: pp. 57, 60 right, 88, 94 left, 97, 117, 145 top (Sports General), 152 right (Acme Newspictures), 156 bottom, 188 bottom, 226, 227; 169 (Fox), 163, 170 (Haas); 60 left, 94 right, 95, 104, 110 bottom, 143 right, 145 bottom (Levick). Rocky Weldon: p. 222. West Side Tennis Club: pp. 39, 40, 43, 82 (U.S. Signal Corps), 87, 137, 142, 152 left, 153 top, 156 top, 162 top, 165, 166 (Fernburger), 167, 176, 177, 184 left (Trostorff), 184 right, 184 bottom (Newbert), 185 (Stoess), 188, 192 right, 194, 197 and 217 (Norris), 208. Wide World Photos: pp. 105, 162 bottom, 173, 174, 175, 186, 187, 223.

The photographs on pp. 45, 48, 49, 206 bottom, and 207 are the author's.

U.S. Library of Congress Cataloging in Publication Data

Minton, Robert, birth date
   Forest Hills: an illustrated history.

   Includes index.
   1. West Side Tennis Club, Forest Hills, N. Y.—
History. 2. Tennis—History.
GV997.W4M55   796.34′2′09747243   75–14461
ISBN–0–397–01094–X

FOR CRONAN AND HELENA

To Ric & Jun —
May the glory that is
Forest Hills endure forever!
Pancho & Billie-Jean
1-28-79

CONTENTS

*Sections of colored photographs
follow pages 80 and 160*

ACKNOWLEDGMENTS

THE HISTORY OF FOREST HILLS is so much part of the history of the West Side Tennis Club that it would have been impossible to put this book together without the enthusiastic cooperation and encouragement of the club's board of governors and a number of members. I would like especially to thank Eugene F. Brady, the president, and Charles W. Tucker, Jr., the vice-president, for arranging many visits to the club and for introductions to members and personnel who patiently answered questions about the club and its development.

Robert A. Burger, the efficient general manager, graciously opened the club's extensive photo files and provided much information about the operation of the U.S. Open. George McGann, the perennial publicity chairman of the Open, was good enough to read the manuscript and correct several errors. Other club members I must thank are Ross and Marney Reid, William P. Mangold, Skip Dewalt, Dr. Edmund Baker, Mrs. Helen Osterrieth and Alexander Epting.

Bill Talbert could not have been more helpful in providing fresh insights into the character of modern professional tennis. Among players who talked freely about Forest Hills were Jaime Fillol, Cliff Sutter, Frank Parker, Vic Seixas, Rod Laver, Harold Solomon, Eddie Dibbs and Ferdi

9

Taygan. Many others spoke out during press conferences, and their candor is appreciated.

The USLTA (now the USTA) opened its library to me, and Pret Hadley, who handles the media corps during the Open, went to great trouble to secure a number of valuable photographs for the book.

Others who contributed to the book include Richard and Katherine Mansfield, Thomas Raleigh, Edward Hickey, Bud Collins, Allison Danzig, Franham Warriner, Edwin Baker, Robert Gray, Warren Woodcock, Spencer Conley, Barry Lorge, Pike Talbert, Harold Zimman, Mrs. Ella Musolino, Harold and Joan Soule, Bruce Old, James W. Sullivan and Mike Blanchard.

Walter Elcock, president of the International Lawn Tennis Association, took time from a busy schedule to share some thoughts with me.

Research was carried out at a number of places: the New York Public Library, the Boston Public Library, the Firestone Library of Princeton University, the Mugar Library of Boston University, the Long Island Historical Society, the Museum of the City of New York, the New York Historical Society, the Racquet Club, the Tennis Hall of Fame, the Boston *Globe* and the archives of Conde Nast. To all those who helped in digging out the facts and the pictures, many, many thanks.

ROBERT MINTON

Concord, Massachusetts
1975

FOREWORD

At Camp Encore, a summer camp in Sweden, Maine, for serious students of music, there is the typical clay tennis court in the woods enclosed with a sagging chicken-wire fence supported by tilting poles. Across the top the kids have put up a large crude sign: FOREST HILLS.

For sixty-one years the national championships and international team matches—Davis Cup and Wightman Cup—have been played at the West Side Tennis Club in the section of Queens Borough, New York, called Forest Hills. This urban setting with the suburban name has long been a synonym for the best tennis in America. To play in a national tournament there is to have reached a measure of excellence beyond the imagination of most of the 34 million who now play tennis in this country. Only a few hundred players in the world are qualified to test themselves on this ground hallowed by Tilden, Wills, Budge, King, Laver and other such greats.

The recent rage that has put tennis ahead of golf as a popular sport has come out of a period of chaos and change in international competition. Open tennis, television and jet planes have allowed promoters to attract hundreds of thousands of spectators and TV audiences of millions, and commercial sponsors have exploited their chances to the full. The public response has been feverish, and eventually the fever may subside. But at the moment Forest Hills is the beneficiary of the national mood and is expecting more people in 1975 than the record crowd of 157,000 at the 1974 Open.

As this book goes to press clay courts are being installed at Forest Hills, one of whose chief charms was its acres of lawn. There may even be matches played under lights at West Side Stadium in 1975. Forest Hills is changing with the times. But what does not change is the quality of its matches.

Tennis is now beginning its second century. Forest Hills is more than a place; it is a tradition. Its history is a large part of the history of tennis itself.

PART I

BEGINNING: 1874-1918

1

TENNIS CAPITAL

"LINESMEN READY? Players ready? Play!"

Plock!

And somewhere on one of twenty-three grass courts of the West Side
Tennis Club the first ball of the 1974 U.S. Open Championships is hit at
Forest Hills. No one pays much attention the first day of the twelve-day
tournament to just what time in the late morning the first match began.
From the uncovered upstairs porch of the clubhouse Lawrence "Skip" Dewalt charts the schedule of matches with a grease pencil on a huge white
plastic board divided into twenty-three squares, calling players over the
public address system.

"Vijay Amritraj, please report to the players' desk."

Four telephones link this command post to various parts of the 12-acre
spread.

"No balls at the Grandstand match!" an assistant on a phone shouts.
"Hank Quinn says Kodes and Creamer are just standing there wondering
why we rushed them." Hank Quinn, tennis pro for Elbow Beach, Bermuda,
is umpiring that match. Cans of balls are dispatched through the 200-yard
maze of pathways to the Grandstand next to the Stadium.

Players on the porch look up at a 747 flying over the apartment houses beyond the Long Island Railroad tracks. The noise momentarily drowns out the sound of jackhammers. A silver train slips by sounding a horn. In front of the clubhouse Arthur Ashe is playing Trey Waltke of St. Louis and winning the third straight set 5–2. On the flagstone terrace the crowd sips drinks and chats, while across the grass, people are standing four deep, absorbed by the match.

Noon, Wednesday, August 28, 1974. They are bunching up outside at the old-fashioned gate with its little red-tile roof at One Tennis Place, a narrow one-way residential street. Club members and players approach the stucco and half-timbered clubhouse on a slate walk lined with beds of geraniums and begonias. This is also the service entrance, and big bags of ice cubes are being shouldered into the various bars within. It is 80 degrees and humid.

Behind screens you can hear tennis balls being hit on clay courts on either side of the entrance. Sarah Palfrey Danzig, national singles champion in 1941 and 1945, is playing mixed doubles in a beat-up white hat, hitting her strokes very slowly, and placing the ball consistently where she wants it to go.

Passing under the red, white and blue bunting at the gate with the okay of Ernie Wolfmann of the Burns Detective Agency, who has worked the Open since it began in 1968 and the nationals for six years before that, is Guillermo Vilas. The Argentine clay-court sensation of the summer is wearing blue jeans, a blue shirt and red beads around his neck, crucifix attached. He spots Isabel Fernandez of Colombia, kisses her on the cheek and chats in Spanish while waiting in the courtyard to register at card tables tended by club member Mrs. Winifred Gordon.

"Thirty dollars, please," she tells each player.

"Take it out of my prize money."

"Okay. You get a free bag." They each take a canvas tennis-gear bag stamped "4711," the name of an eau de cologne that has been declared "official refreshant of the U.S. Open."

Players are crowding in, carrying their gear. Most are in sports clothes. Björn Borg, the Swedish idol, comes in without fanfare wearing green corduroy slacks and a light green sport shirt. Many have come by subway after a night at the Summit Hotel, at Lexington Avenue and 51st Street, where 250 contestants, managers, journalists and others related to the Open have been given a special $18 room rate.

From One Tennis Place the club at Forest Hills is unimposing and unpretentious. No sweeping driveway, no pillared porte cochere, no uniformed attendants—just busboys in white shirts and black trousers showing up for work. Space in New York is measured in square feet. For elegance and spaciousness you need the expanse of Westchester County or the Main Line. The West Side Tennis Club's clubhouse is purely functional, a place to change clothes, shower, have a meal, play a game of cards.

The luxury is the courts—sixty clay, twenty-three grass—available from 8 A.M., when the locker room boys arrive, until sunset. For some members the Open is a bother, that time of year when courts are preempted by the tournament, by strangers—umpires, newsmen, schoolchildren, God knows who.

But the big tournaments bring the gate receipts that provide so handsomely for members. Maximum dues are $600 a year. Initiation fees are $800, and less for certain classes of members. Members know how much it would cost to belong without the Open. And most are enormously proud to host the biggest event in American tennis.

For Forest Hills is America's tennis capital. Since 1914 more important tennis matches have been played on the grass courts of the West Side Tennis Club than anywhere in the United States, and they have drawn more spectators overall because there is no other facility of its size in this country devoted strictly to tennis. The location of a tennis capital in residential Queens, Long Island, one of New York's five boroughs, is no more anomalous than the location of the capital of New York State in Albany or of the capital of Pennsylvania in Harrisburg. American capitals have not evolved as they have in the Old World; they have been deliberately established—often only after a bitter struggle. Forest Hills is no exception.

Wimbledon became the world capital of tennis naturally because after tennis grew popular in the 1870s, the All-England Cricket Club in the London suburb of Wimbledon was the leading place where tennis was played, and it was there that the rules of tennis were drawn up. Its annual fortnight of tournament matches became the world championships. And while these were being played, Forest Hills was simply farmland. Long Island was much as Walt Whitman described it in *Specimen Days:*

> I have often been out on the edges of these plains toward sundown,
> and can yet recall in fancy the interminable cow processions, and
> hear the music of the tin or copper bells clanking far or near, and
> breathe the cool of the sweet and slightly aromatic evening air,
> and note the sunset.

At that time America's tennis capital was that sybaritic watering place Newport, Rhode Island. Before Forest Hills could wrest from Newport the privilege of staging the national championships, it had to prove itself worthy of this, the highest distinction that the United States Lawn Tennis Association can confer. From 1881 to 1914 the Newport Casino clung jealously to this honor and resisted with all the tenacity of an old champion the challenge of an upstart club that had been organized only in 1892 and never had grass courts until 1908.

Once Forest Hills had won the struggle over Newport it became America's Wimbledon, the site of the national championships and many Davis Cup and Wightman Cup matches. Though challenged in the early years by the Germantown Cricket Club of Philadelphia, it has retained its title as the center of championship tennis in the western hemisphere.

The 1974 United States Open Championships drew the biggest crowds in history, 157,000 people in twelve days, and the TV audience during four

17

days of telecasting was 10 million each day. Gate receipts exceeded $900,000. Tennis had become the fastest-growing spectator sport in a country that is so sports-crazy that even something called box lacrosse can gain acceptance. Despite the proliferation of tournaments arising out of the fantastic growth of professional tennis, the U.S. Open at Forest Hills stands out as the most prestigious—if not the most lucrative for the players.

"It's now the most important tournament in the world," Rod Laver said during the 1974 Volvo International at Bretton Woods, New Hampshire, "because it's the last leg." It comes at the end of the summer, after the Australian, French and British championships. As two-time winner of the Grand Slam, consisting of these three and the U.S. championship, Laver thinks of Forest Hills in terms of the climax, the last of four tournaments that clearly establish world supremacy in tennis. Now thirty-six and a millionaire, Laver chose not to compete at Forest Hills in 1974. But when Jimmy Connors so overwhelmingly defeated Rosewall in the U.S. Open finals and mentioned he would like to meet Laver in a match, he was conferring on himself what Forest Hills tacitly gave him: world championship.

Don Budge, the first person to win the Grand Slam, said: "Winning at Wimbledon was wonderful and it meant a lot to me. But there is nothing quite like winning the championship of your own country. That's what counts the most with anybody." Especially from the perspective of this side of the Atlantic, Wimbledon with all its prestige and genteel tradition seems far off in time and space by September, and Forest Hills then becomes in the late season the leading symbol of all that is meant by greatness in tennis.

> There is nothing spectacular in the few acres of lawn, parking space, grandstand and playing surface that make up the site of the national tennis championships. The short leafy approach to the West Side clubhouse barely muffles the sound of auto traffic, barely screens the nearby apartment houses, delicatessens, movie theatres and used-car lots. During a tense exchange on the court when the crowd is silent you can almost hear the rumble of the Queens subway under the boulevard just a block away. Yet, when a tennis player leaves the weathered brown 1920s Tudor pile of a building that is the clubhouse, walks through the dining porch onto the terrace where a few people sit over their tall drinks, and starts down the neatly edged path toward the courts, he is as remote from the world of traffic and commerce as if he were on a Caribbean island whose only interests are sports and sun. He is in the very capital of the world of tennis, and he is a member of its privileged class.

Billy Talbert wrote this in 1958 in his autobiography, *Playing for Life*. The three-time national doubles champion and two-time national singles finalist probably has more feeling for Forest Hills than any other top player. Partly as a result of this obvious affection for what he now considers "a very inadequate facility for staging something as spectacular as the U.S. Open," Talbert has been since 1970 its chairman and tournament director. He operates during the matches from a shanty of an office with one window on the Stadium court; for him Forest Hills is largely an endless series of telephone conversations and conferences with tournament referee Mike Blanchard and various club and USLTA officials as he runs a show that grossed $1.5 million from all sources in 1974. He is certainly not remote from the world of traffic ("we only have parking space for 300 cars, and the one-way streets are terrible for cabs") and commerce ("the equal prizes for women are hard to justify when there are twice as many men playing"), but he is rather remote from most of the actual matches, especially during the hectic early rounds, when he has time only for brief glimpses of play in the Stadium. He emerges from time to time, wearing a bright yellow sport shirt and crimson slacks, to preside over little ceremonies between Stadium matches, such as the presentation to Betsy Nagelson of the most-promising-young-player award of 1974.

Talbert never turned pro and has pursued a successful business career with the United States Banknote Corporation, of which he is now senior vice-president. He takes no recompense for the enormous administrative work involved in the U.S. Open and is psychologically out of phase with the monied world of professional tennis of today, deploring the paying of umpires and ball boys and exasperated by the demands of the players. Yet it is Talbert who has kept Forest Hills at the top in prize money. No tournament has exceeded the U.S. Open's huge grand total of $271,720 in 1974. The players may grumble about the courts or about the quality of life in New York, but there are few complaints about the size of the purse Talbert gets together through a number of shrewd ventures—from naming "4711" the official refreshant to renting tent space to Pepsi-Cola, Phillip Morris, *Family Circle, Sports Illustrated* and other companies for lunches and cocktail parties.

The importance of making Forest Hills pay off cannot be overstated. The USLTA depends on the Open as its chief source of revenue ($200,000 in 1974) to carry out an extensive program of amateur development and tournament sponsorship across the country. Amateur tennis is dead at the highest levels of competition, but just below the pros are the college players who spend the rest of their lives competing in local, state and sometimes national events. Forest Hills indirectly subsidizes this activity, which includes fifty-four major championship tournaments and is carried out by a network of seventeen regional sections.

And then, of course, the West Side Tennis Club, which owns "Forest Hills," owns the 12 acres of courts, the Stadium and the clubhouse, benefits substantially from its historic promotion of top tennis. The club is non-profit, but the $150,000 it received after taxes in 1974 makes it possible to keep dues for its 1,200 members below those of most clubs. Without this income the average dues would be up to $1,600. Furthermore, the capital value of the place, which cost little more than $250,000, is estimated to be

$10 million! But its true value is in its location. Where in New York today could you find the space for another Forest Hills, located next to a railway station and three blocks from a subway, fifteen minutes from mid-Manhattan?

Convenience of location is certainly one of the chief attractions of Forest Hills and the reason in the first place that the area was developed into an exclusive suburban community called Forest Hills Gardens. The subway makes it quite feasible for spectators to come to the Open during lunch, stay a few hours and still go back to the office if they must, or at least get back to town in time to commute home at the usual hour. The Open, coming at the end of vacation days and before the beginning of the football season, catches the New York crowd in a transitional mood, nostalgic for the countryside they spent their vacation in and eager for a few more hours in the sun. Forest Hills, though, is not an oasis in early September, when the humidity is often 90 percent and higher. Yet something compels people to leave air-conditioned offices and come out on the hottest of days to this emerald plantation of delicate turf.

The grass is an important part of the pleasure principle. People come just to look at the acres of courts, which until now have been all grass in the center with clay on the periphery. Will they still be as thrilled by the changeover to clay in 1975? End of an era, some moan. But those who have learned to live with Astroturf will adjust to the green Har-tru clay that is going in at Forest Hills. Some grass courts will remain for members, as at Longwood, where new clay courts drew no adverse comment from record crowds at the 1974 U.S. Pro Championship tournament.

The decision to go to clay for the 1975 Open was inevitable and was even promised for 1974. As late as August that year Rod Laver was saying, "They'll never take the grass up at Forest Hills!" And the man who lost to him in the finals at Bretton Woods, Harold Solomon, was saying, "The grass must go." And Solomon was right. The majority of players prefer clay to grass and a hard surface to clay. During the 1974 Open the players' Association of Tennis Professionals voted for something called Plexi-pave, an asphalt composition that can be of varied roughness according to the speed of bounce desired. Their wishes remain just wishes. To the members already playing on clay, clay is easier on the feet than asphalt.

Clifford Sutter, who ranked third in 1932 and grew up in New Orleans playing on clay, came to see how challenging grass is, with its possibilities for subtle drop shots and slices which there is no time for on slower surfaces. Now an executive for Bancroft Sporting Goods Company, he shakes his head sadly at the thought of the interminable rallies that lie ahead at Forest Hills.

Even as Bill Tilden played at Forest Hills in the twenties, he foresaw the end of lawn tennis because of the cost of maintenance. No amount of money can provide grass courts today that will withstand the pounding of several hundred top players. Within a few hours the soft turf is torn and worn, and the bounces are heartbreaking. In 1974 it rained frequently in the

To dramatize the tie breaker at the U.S. Open, a red flag with the initials S D *for sudden death is hoisted outside the photographers' booth at West Side Stadium.*

evening, making the grass so slippery that one senior player, Dick Savitt, who ranked third in 1957, was taken away in an ambulance after sliding into a fence and wrecking his shoulder.

"It's plain mud!" Irish grounds keeper Owney Sheridan groaned in disgust, pronouncing it *mood*, as in *hood*. "They shouldn' be playin'."

But tournaments have to be played continuously, and good clay courts dry out in a few hours. Ironically, the reason Forest Hills cannot develop hard lawn courts like those at Wimbledon is that they would require more clay than New York weather would support. Because of the semitropical heat, adding more clay to the soil holding the turf would cause the roots to bake and wither. Hence Forest Hills turf grows in a sandy soil that gives it a lovely spongy feel, but is too fragile to hold up under the slam-bang serve-and-volley game of today's tennis. At cool Wimbledon the clay under the turf almost gives it the solid feel of a clay court.

The players seldom play on grass now except in England and Australia. The Eastern grass-court circuit is optional and may simply disappear once the championships are played on clay. European players have always played on clay. Much of the best American tennis has come out of the South and California, where hard courts are used exclusively. Indoor tennis is played on everything from wood to linoleum as well as clay, but never on grass. So in the one-hundredth year of lawn tennis, the lawn disappeared.

"The customers get more for their money on clay," Laver says. "I always felt at Forest Hills I was gypping them because the points were over quickly."

On grass the ball bounces fastest and inhibits the return of serve, so that the server can come in for the volley with great assurance. But on clay the ball bounces slowly giving the receiver time to really smack his return, thus beginning what is often a long baseline duel, beloved by the crowds.

But this is truer of men's than of women's tennis. Women cannot hit the ball with anywhere near the velocity that men can, so they cannot come in behind their serves with much assurance. And so we have seen in women's matches at Forest Hills often the best tennis to watch. The grace of Evonne Goolagong's ground strokes from deep behind the baseline as she out-hit Chris Evert in the semifinals of the 1974 Open was an exquisite delight, distinctly different from the almost terrifying feeling aroused by the devastating two-handed backhand drives of Jimmy Connors against Rosewall in the finals. With clay we will see more ground strokes by the men, but we will miss the feel of the balletlike grass game played by the women. Clay is harsh and abrasive, lacking in the aesthetic appeal of grass, which is an organic, growing thing, redolent with freshness, virginal, domestic, and of a deep color that symbolizes fertility. Clay hardly allows for the dink shot that stops dead on grass. You can slide into short shots on clay, and furthermore the ball will rise.

The question of court surfaces is really not a major issue among spectators, just among the players themselves, some of whom play better on one surface than on another. It has been proven that crowds will watch good tennis on anything, including a city street. For in the end it is the contest, the struggle, that grips the onlooker, not the artistry or the beauty. Who would pay money to see Evert and Goolagong merely rally from the baseline for an hour without playing a match?

In West Side Stadium, an intimate horseshoe bowl holding 15,000, there is something of the quality of the original Olympic games in ancient Greece. A reverence that approaches a religious feeling seems to develop in the silence, broken by murmurs, sighs, "ohs" and "ahs" of wonderment at the retrievals, the smashes, the net-cord shots. A singles match can be seen as a battle of Titans, of athletic gods, or as a Promethean defiance of the fates that limit man. "The contest is only a game," said Charles J. Ping, provost of Central Michigan University, commenting on athletics in *The Chronicle of Higher Education*, September 23, 1974, "yet the charged air, the sense of conflict and resolution of conflict, the joy and the anguish have an electric effect on all who are caught up in the moment."

The players seem at times to be acting out for all of us our yearnings to surpass ourselves in their straining for mastery. And this can be seen in the curious psychology of crowd preference. Moved by sympathy for an underdog or by antipathy to what they consider the inappropriate behavior of a player, spectators will switch favorites in an instant. The crowds turned against Chris Evert in 1974 and rooted for Evonne Goolagong, but when Billie Jean King lost the first set of the finals to Evonne, some of the crowd went over to Billie Jean, and by the last games of the third set, when the tension became almost unbearable and there actually were tears in peoples' eyes (for joy? gratitude?), the Stadium seemed evenly divided, as if no one wanted either to win, so magnificent was the playing of both women, so moving the spirit of determination of each. When the president of the USLTA presented the cup after the match and maladroitly said, "I knew all along Billie Jean would win," the crowd booed and Billie Jean ducked into the Granada sedan she had won.

"I was embarrassed," she told the press. She also said, "I can't tell you how I won." Winning is not quite everything, and the winner has often a deep feeling for the loser, the partner who made victory possible, so to speak.

There is something awesome about playing the Stadium, contestants say. Great players like Stan Smith are irked when they are scheduled in the Grandstand rather than the Stadium, where they believe they play a better game under better conditions. Ferdi Taygan, a coming young player from UCLA, entered at Forest Hills for the first time in 1974 and was startled to find that he would play a first-round match with the ninth seed, Vilas, in the Stadium.

"I was very nervous at first," he said, "and I dropped the first two sets. And then I settled down and took the next two sets." He lost the final set 6–3, but he had stretched Vilas, who later lost to Ashe in straight sets in the fourth round. "It had something to do with Forest Hills," Taygan explained later. "I love this place." He hung around long enough to reach the third round of the men's doubles, when he and Bruce Manson lost to Cornejo and Fillol, eventual finalists.

They say that Forest Hills has changed, that it is no longer a place of gentility and decorum, that professionalism has spoiled the players, and World Team Tennis has spoiled the spectators. It is amazing, though, how little has changed. The Stadium, the courts, the clubhouses are all as they were. Booths have been set up under the Stadium, creating an atmosphere of a bazaar; the Open Club has been created there as a private refuge for those who can afford the $75 fee and want the privilege of uncrowded rest rooms, a place to sit down for lunch or a drink between matches; the press box has been air-conditioned. And that is all. Otherwise Forest Hills is the same place Tilden played at. Even in his day spectators were not always polite and players bullied the umpires with gestures and frowns.

What *has* changed is the community of Forest Hills itself. It became a typical New York apartment community during the thirties, when the subway was extended there, and high rises now dominate the landscape. The area has been wracked by a bitter controversy about low-cost housing. And since the introduction of jet planes the noise level, always high because of passing Long Island Railroad trains, has risen. As many as one plane per minute may pass over the Stadium at times during a match.

The crowds, of course, are bigger. There used to be a couple of thousand on opening day only a few years ago. In 1974 there were 13,000. And how they dress! At the first Davis Cup matches in 1914 the men wore dark wool suits and boaters, and the ladies' dresses were voluminous and long-sleeved. Now the entire gamut of modern garb may be seen at Forest Hills —from cut-off jeans to the highest fashions. Some of the older umpires still wear business suits and straw hats, but not boaters, and there are young businessmen in button-down shirts and striped ties. But the casual look predominates: men without jackets in tennis shirts which they may take off for a sunbath, girls in shorts or tennis costumes, and thousands wearing paper visors provided by Planters' Mr. Peanut, who wears a top hat and stands inside a plastic peanut passing them out.

During the 1974 Open an alert observer would have seen the president of Princeton University, William Bowen, a former Ohio tennis champion, scurrying under the Grandstand in sports clothes carrying a jug of lemonade. Nearby, in a large planter's straw hat, the comedian Alan King was hanging over the fence watching a match.

Elegant the scene is not. The players wear what they please. John Newcombe sports a pink shirt that somehow makes him seem less formidable. Billie Jean wears her Liberty Bell dress to advertise the Philadelphia team she played for. Colorful the scene certainly is, and however *un*tennislike by old standards it may look, spectators clearly know more about the game than ever. Television has taught them who the best players are and what the dramatic moments are likely to be, and as a result, for the first time, the unreserved seats in the Stadium were oversold in 1974.

"We could get away with overselling in the past because enough people were wandering around outside looking at other matches," a ticket salesman said. "But now more people want to see the featured players because they've seen 'em on the tube."

The growth in the number of tennis players, estimated at 34 million now, has been accompanied by a growth in the sophistication and extent of media coverage of tennis in general and Forest Hills in particular. CBS Tennis Classic matches go on all summer, and the Public Broadcasting System covers top tournaments for viewers, who not only see matches but watch the players being interviewed and hear their own analysis discussed by former tournament players like Donald Dell and Tony Trabert. Printed programs sold at tournaments are slick, sophisticated and readable, and three monthlies, *Tennis, World Tennis* and *Tennis U.S.A.*, have mass circulation. All this means that spectators are likely to be fairly expert witnesses of what is going on on the court.

"I wish it were like it used to be when you could hear a pin drop!" a woman exclaimed at the 1974 Open when the crowd was whistling at a bad call. "No one in the Stadium ever dared question a call." This is non-history. Crowds have given the umpires a bad time at least since World War I. In 1919 the National Umpires Association had to issue a public statement asking crowds to give umpires a break, not to applaud errors and to withhold applause during rallies. Tilden was notorious for his rough treatment of linesmen.

Fans are largely justified in vociferating when a call is bad. Many linesmen are not young. If Pancho Gonzales at forty-six, after winning the 1974 Grand Masters at Forest Hills, can say, "My eyes are not so good any more. I can't see at the net like I used to," then how good is the vision of linesmen in their sixties?

World Team Tennis, which encourages rooting for the team throughout a match, is said to have broken spectator discipline elsewhere. A little, perhaps, but how influential is team tennis when teams draw only a couple of thousand spectators? And all the returns are not in on World Team Tennis, which in the aggregate reportedly cost backers $300,000 in losses. It certainly has not turned the West Side Stadium into a ball park. You still *can* hear a pin drop at crucial moments—providing no train or plane is passing by. Crowds still express themselves more by applause than by roaring. The nature of tennis limits the degree of noise, even in team tennis. Part of the pleasure of watching a match is hearing the sounds of the ball—on the racket strings, on the court, against the net. A serve that ticks the net cord is generally heard by the crowd. A wood shot is identified by its inappropriate sound. For a bland experience, turn down the TV sound while you're watching tennis. There are nuances of sound: metal rackets are more twangy than wood, and a slice is quieter than a flat stroke. On grass, feet thud. On clay there is the sound of sliding.

And the players are mostly silent. They groan, grunt, puff (when Newcombe serves he sounds like a steam engine starting up as the air rushes out of him). They also talk aloud to themselves occasionally. Billie Jean is constantly scolding herself. But players say little to each other and become vocal only over a bad call. Since man is an imitator, spectators tend to be quiet. When they do get noisy, they respond quickly to the umpire's dignified request to "settle down."

Forest Hills has not changed essentially. It just has become more of what it was. It provides more good tennis at the Open than ever could be seen in amateur days. For example, in his first match in 1974 Stan Smith had to face Jaime Fillol, the Chilean champ, and was lucky to win in five sets on a tie breaker. Such matches draw bigger crowds to early rounds now, and it is not so easy to move on the narrow flower-bordered paths during the first days. Security has had to be tightened to keep people out of places they have no tickets or badges for. Chris Evert herself could not get into the Stadium marquee to watch her fiancé, Jimmy Connors, play one day because she forgot her pass. Instead of raising a fuss, she walked back to the clubhouse. Because she had no ticket, John Alexander's beautiful wife was actually kicked out of the marquee while watching her husband play Connors.

Despite such impersonality, Forest Hills retains a sense of intimacy. Name players wander among the crowds, noticed but not always pestered by autograph-crazy kids. Ilie Nastase leans on the fence at the Grandstand

25

carrying his rackets and loops of gut, watching Smith and Fillol until his own match is called. Tom Okker, in jeans, strolls about the courts taking in the scene.

Bud Collins, the TV commentator and Boston *Globe* columnist, chats with Donald Dell and Jack Kramer under the Stadium—with no TV cameras on them. After a day of this sort of thing an observer remarked, "I almost feel like saying hello to all these players. I've seen so much of them, I think I know them." And there goes Don Budge in tennis clothes—a bit heavy, but still playing exhibition tennis. And there, smoking a pipe and wearing a press badge on his dark suit, is Fred Perry, part of the British newspaper corps.

"When is Forest Hills going to get over its snobbery?" a girl was overheard asking during a lull in a match. Is Forest Hills snobbish? A snob affects an attitude of superiority he is not entitled to. But Forest Hills represents true superiority in tennis. There is nothing pretentious about Forest Hills at all. The West Side Tennis Club is of course exclusive, like any club. But all it offers is tennis, tennis, tennis. When a member wanted to donate a quarter-million-dollar swimming pool to the club, the Board of Governors turned it down. It's a tennis club, period. A pool would muck things up. Too many kids would make too much noise splashing around. A pool would complicate the club's simple mission: to provide first-class tennis for its members and the best tennis in the world once a year for the public.

The story of this mission, how it began and what it has accomplished, is the subject of what follows.

2

TENNIS ON MANHATTAN'S WEST SIDE

Tennis arrived in the United States via New York harbor in 1874, when Mary Ewing Outerbridge of Staten Island landed from Bermuda with a package containing paraphernalia so unusual that it was held up by customs before she could set it up a few weeks later. She had discovered tennis while visiting her brother, Sir Joseph Outerbridge, on the estate of Sir Brownlow Gray, and she brought back a net, rackets and balls with a set of instructions.

This game had little relation to whatever it was that Peter Stuyvesant as the Dutch governor of New Amsterdam banned on October 15, 1659—the first instance of something called tennis being played in what became New York. That ban must have been effective. No one had the slightest idea what Miss Outerbridge's game was all about, and her own knowledge was rudimentary.

Lawn tennis was adapted from the ancient game of court tennis, which appeared in Europe at the end of the Middle Ages and became a great fashion in the seventeenth and eighteenth centuries. It then died out after the French Revolution, which by chance had its inception in a court-tennis court at Versailles built in 1686. The essentials of court tennis are racket, ball, net and a complex indoor court. The rules are so involved that players require someone to keep score and look after the balls. This function was performed by a servant in ancient times, and the word *serve*, meaning to put the ball in play, probably reflects a situation in which a servant was asked for a ball to get things started.

What Miss Outerbridge saw on the lawn of Clermont, Sir Brownlow's Bermuda estate, was a new game called Sphairistike (meaning "ball play" in Greek), which was promoted by a man more publicized today than in his own time, Major Walter Clopton Wingfield. Had his name been Smith, would tennis scholars have been so assiduous in attributing the invention of lawn tennis to him? Wingfield patented his game on February 23, 1874, twenty-one days after Miss Outerbridge reached New York. He had already introduced at Nantclwyd, Wales, a game that had been played for at least five years in northern England. This "sticky," as his game was known, had some curious characteristics, the most striking being an hourglass-shaped court, making the width of the baseline 30 feet while the net was only 21 feet across. This innovation was modeled after an indoor badminton court in India, where badminton originated. (The name is taken from the country seat of the Duke of Beaufort, Badminton, Gloucestershire.) Because a door entering the court swung inward in the center, the width of the net had been adjusted accordingly. To have reversed the direction of the door would no doubt have created a greater inconvenience, the nature of which was never recorded.

Anyone who thought he could get away with making people play a game called sticky on a court requiring players to adjust their shots to receding sidelines deserves some measure of oblivion, and this was accorded Wingfield in his obituary in the *Times* in 1912, which neglected to list Sphairistike among his achievements. This editorial lapse has since been redressed by sportswriters, although the Leamington Club outside Birmingham makes the claim of having the first lawn-tennis court in 1868. But Wingfield is consistently credited as the father of lawn tennis. The official bulletin of the New England Lawn Tennis Association states:

> The game, as the invention of an Englishman, Maj. Walter Clopton
> Wingfield, was first played in December, 1873, at a garden party
> at Nantclwyd, Wales.

A double fault should be called. The game had already been played obscurely for several years in England, and no one can be said to have invented a game that evolved over centuries. See, for example, the portrait of Charles IX as an infant, holding a tennis racket in 1552. Wingfield was not the father of modern tennis, but he was a midwife. He was a high-class promoter. He even succeeded in getting the Prince of Wales to play sticky.

"He is the man who inspired, if not sired, the sport," Laurie Pignon of the London *Daily Mail* has written.

The refinement of rubber was a chief factor in the development of lawn tennis. The ball had to be soft enough not to damage the grass yet have the liveliness imparted by rubber, a substance only vulcanized in 1839. Other important contributions of nineteenth-century industry were the wealth that created a new leisure class and railroads that carried its members to their country estates. Bermuda, Staten Island, Nahant, Massachusetts, and Newport, Rhode Island, were the places associated with the earliest development of American tennis—not New York, Chicago or Los Angeles. An upper-class stamp was put on the game by court tennis's long tradition as the sport of kings and by the character of the game itself: it is limited to two or four people, who take up considerable space, which requires expensive maintenance. Handball is a more plebeian sport because it can be played against any handy wall.

> Hardly a firehouse in New York existed without a friendly but high-spirited game going on during the few leisure hours afforded to engine company members.

So states the *Sports Almanac* in discussing the introduction of that game from Ireland in the late nineteenth century.

It is not the lawn that makes lawn tennis expensive; it is the cost of any court that is limited to singles or doubles that makes it a luxury. In the same space, one or two basketball games can be played by ten to twenty players, who need buy no racket or tennis balls at $3 for a can of three.

Certainly money was no problem when Miss Outerbridge got permission to set up a court on a corner of the Staten Island Cricket and Baseball Club grounds, and it was not long before other lawn courts made their appearance in the East. In the West the first concrete courts were installed in Santa Monica, California, in 1879.

The name *lawn tennis* has been attributed to the British statesman Arthur Balfour, author of the Balfour Declaration, a chief basis for Israel's claim of sovereignty. But certainly, outside of England and Australia, clay quickly became the logical surface for tennis. Less logical was the variety of rules. The game could be played by two, four or eight on any piece of turf marked out on the spur of the moment. One set of rules stated that if the receiver touched a bad serve, the server got the point automatically. Atavistically today the idea persists that it is unfair to the server to hit a bad ball. (Laver says, when in doubt hit any serve!) The game was scored by single points, like squash, ending at 15. The net drooped from 5-foot posts to a height of 4 feet in the center. In 1877, only three years after Wingfield patented the game, the British drew up what essentially are the present rules of the game, and on May 21, 1881, the United States National Lawn Tennis Association was formed in New York by nineteen clubs, fifteen of which were represented by proxy, and none were west of Pittsburgh. Among the founders was E. H. Outerbridge, Mary's brother. The rules of the All-England Club at Wimbledon were at that time adopted by the association.

The first men's national championships were held in August 1881 at the Newport Casino, an elegant new club built out of spite by James Gordon Bennett, the flamboyant publisher of the New York *Herald*. On a bet, a guest of his named Captain Candy, a member of the visiting British polo team, had ridden a horse into the ultra-exclusive men's club called the Reading Room, and his guest's privileges were promptly revoked. The stuffiness of the Reading Room was taken as a personal affront by Bennett, who thought Newport needed a new, gay social center.

The Casino, designed by Charles McKim and Stanford White, brought the European idea of a social center to America for the first time. There was a dance twice weekly in the ballroom, concerts on an open bandstand called the Piazza, and a great field of lush lawn-tennis courts and a grandstand overlooking the courts where America's nationals were played for thirty-four successive years.

In New York, tennis was making its appearance in Central Park. Informal grass courts gave way to smoother clay courts with fences, but there were not enough of them for the hundreds of New Yorkers eager to play. Clubs were springing up in the suburbs. The Brookline Country Club outside of Boston was the first club of its kind, built in 1882. The Country Club of Westchester County appeared in 1884, and tennis was its *raison d'être*. But country clubs, though based on some sport, particularly golf, filled a social need for the well-to-do. Caspar Whitney explained it in *Evolution of the Country Club* (Boston, 1928):

> The country club has given Americans a club and country villa combined in one, where having practically all the comforts and delights of housekeeping they are called upon to assume none of its cares or responsibilities. For the stewards attend to the early morning market, worries with the servants, and may be held to account for the shortcomings of the chef and at a cost below that on which a separate establishment of equal appointment could be maintained.

He was describing an expensive cooperative venture to help fill up leisure time with exercise and agreeable social activities. During Prohibition, of course, some of them became glorified saloons, and their image suffered accordingly.

Tennis clubs, at least at their inception, were started because of the insufficiency of public courts. Local governments were not prepared to meet the recreational demands of tennis players when the game first appeared. Basketball, baseball, football, track and swimming have been publicly subsidized because of the larger numbers served by the facilities. One tennis court used for twelve hours for doubles, bringing in new players hourly, can serve only forty-eight people. Schedule one basketball game an hour on the same space and you serve a hundred and twenty. Baseball, football and soccer require more space, but the teams are bigger. Six or eight turn out for the high school tennis team, fifty for football. Only golf is more cost-intensive than tennis. To this day in Central Park players appear at dawn to sign up for a court.

Not every club began as the Newport Casino did, backed by a fortune.

There were thirteen original members who organized the West Side Tennis Club on April 22, 1892, and their modest aim was to rent ground on Central Park West, between 88th and 89th Streets, for three clay courts, which were opened June 11. The officers were Charles B. Collins, president, E. C. Hebbard, vice-president, and Stephen C. Millett, secretary-treasurer. Before the season was over, the membership had risen to forty-three and the number of courts to five. In an eight-hour period every member would theoretically have a chance to play.

The claim was that these were among the finest clay courts in the world, and from the one existing photograph it is apparent that at least the "championship court," running east and west, was laid out spaciously, with ample room between baseline and fences—the so-called backroom or runback—and plenty of room on the sides. The two north-and-south courts had less than 10 feet beyond the baseline, and to play these courts required some expertise in the half volley. A so-called clubhouse consisted of a shed with two dressing rooms and cold showers. The club put its money into tennis and not into social facilities. There were plenty of places for drinking, eating and dancing, but what the city needed was a good tennis court. This single-minded concentration on having an excellent place to play tennis rather than a showplace presented the starkest contrast to the Newport concept of display.

The West Side Tennis Club began as a men's club. There were no family memberships and there still are none. To this day women must join separately; their number is limited to 165 out of 590 active members and they have no vote. There was a $10 initiation fee and dues were $10 a year. Membership was restricted on the basis of congeniality and the ability to play a good game of tennis. That tennis at the West Side was first class can be seen by glancing at the number of its players who ranked among the top ten in the country.

The USLTA* began ranking players in 1885. Among the members of the club in the top ten in the early days were E. P. Fischer, S. C. Millett, J. P. Paret (ranked number three in 1899), J. A. Allen, F. B. Alexander (ranked number three in 1908), H. H. Hackett and R. D. Little. Alexander and Hackett are members of the Tennis Hall of Fame in Newport. The quality of play in the first club tournament in June 1894 was said to be as good as anywhere in the country. In 1897 the USLTA gave the club the privilege of holding the city-wide Metropolitan Championships.

This may seem insignificant in the history of tennis, but it must be remembered that the USLTA, an organization that has taken a great deal of abuse from players and the press, had already become the only unifying force in American tennis. It had and retains two enormous powers, the official ranking of players and the official sanctioning of tournaments. These

* It was the USNLTA until 1920, when the N for "National" was dropped. In 1975, after Forest Hills replaced much of its grass with clay, the L was dropped, and now it's just the USTA—United States Tennis Association.

functions are essential to creating an orderly framework for developing competition among top players. When a governing body of tennis loses its authority, anarchy follows. In 1972 top players were able to boycott Wimbledon. One of the great fears at Forest Hills is of a boycott that would turn off the crowds and ruin the Open financially. For better or worse, the USLTA ran top tennis with an iron hand when the amateurs were supreme. So to have the city championships on the West Side courts confirmed a status the club had quickly acquired through the quality of its matches.

Tennis, of course, had not developed the sophistication that came during the next generation, but it had long ago left behind the gentle game played in blazers, the days when an underhand serve was used. That serve, by the way, is not entirely ineffective. A good player who develops arm trouble can put the ball in play in doubles with an underhand serve and still place it in the corners or deep enough to prevent the receiver from scoring a winner with his return. Many weekend players today are deceived by the advantage of a good overhand serve, which requires considerable practice and self-discipline. An underhand serve that goes in is better than an overhand serve that is a fault! Early champions soon learned the importance of placement and the use of spin both in attacking and defending.

The great Bill Tilden was born in 1893, and at the age of eight he was beating boys twice his age by watching older players. His all-court game may have been the result of an eclectic style that included both the older and the newer ways of playing. He was willing to use any stroke that was effective and to change one that was not. Only in the matter of tactics was he a bit of a purist. The big game of serve and volley developed by Jack Kramer did not suit Tilden because he preferred to hit ground strokes. In volleying there is seldom time to stroke the ball. You must meet it and place it quickly. The early players figured out all sorts of ingenious contortions to allow maximum spin and keep the ball in the court and make it bounce in ways to throw their opponent's timing off. They took the net less often.

The rackets of the day were a couple of ounces heavier than the average 14½ ounces, handles were thicker and the baseline was occupied more often than the net. But already dozens of books on how to play the game had been published and there were elaborate theories on tactics. One was "center theory": Play as many shots as you can deep in the center because your opponent cannot angle the ball very much. The grip was debated. An Irish player, H. F. Lawford, created a following in the 1880s for holding the racket face horizontal to the ground, which was actually forerunner of the Western grip. Lawford also suggested taking the hook out of the racket shape and making it a perfect oval, since the dip in the rim of the court-tennis racket was an aid in trapping the half volley, an infrequent lawn-tennis stroke.

A further refinement of Lawford's was advocating a shift of the seam of the tennis ball from the outside (as in baseball) to the inside. As late as 1927 Charles LaRue, a tennis theorist, was predicting widespread adoption of the Lawford grip. At the same time the Eastern grip, with the racket head vertical to the ground, was becoming almost universal in the United States, and the continental-grip compromise of these radically opposed grips was gaining acceptance in Europe.

Just how many people in the country played tennis before 1900 is unknown, but a sporting-goods industry had developed after the Bancroft brothers started their racket factory in Pawtucket, Rhode Island, in 1882, followed by Spalding Brothers and Wright & Ditson. (Bancroft, now in Woonsocket, Rhode Island, still makes its rackets largely by hand and uses 260 different operations to complete its best model.) Rackets were named after top players, whose pictures appeared on cards in Richmond Straight Cut smoking tobacco along with those of baseball players. Champions like R. D. Sears and H. W. Slocum, Jr., were aristocratic amateurs sowing the seeds of professional endorsement.

Eventually tennis made its appearance on the grounds of the White House. Only Teddy Roosevelt could have inspired the following from A. Wallis Myers in his book *The Complete Lawn Tennis Player* (1908):

> At Washington, the seat of government, it enjoys unusual prestige; not only the public officials but the President and several members of the cabinet being numbered among its ardent adherents. Mr. Roosevelt personally supervised the construction of a hard-packed clay court in a corner of the White House grounds, not forgetting to add a dark green fence which should serve the double purpose of a playing background and screen.

T.R. was said to play nearly every afternoon with a coterie dubbed the Tennis Cabinet. Among guest players once was the Bishop of London.

In 1892 the West Side Tennis Club had been fortunate to find a vacant lot to rent on Central Park West. Ten years later, as population pressure encouraged apartment house construction, the property became too valuable to use for tennis, and the club was obliged to move near Columbia University at 117th Street, between Morningside Drive and Amsterdam Avenue. The property had room for eight courts, of which four were constructed at first. The rent was $20 per court per year! This very uncommercial price was arrived at because the owner, Mrs. John Drexel of the Philadelphia banking family, hardly needed the money and wanted to do a favor for some charming people in New York. She apparently knew nothing about tennis. The savings allowed the club to redo a house on the grounds, this time with hot showers.

Of the club's 110 members, some were prominent. The president was Dr. James Ewing, a pathologist teaching at Cornell Medical School who became one of the country's leading authorities on cancer. Sheppard Homans, Jr., had been a great halfback for Princeton. Such men felt the club now needed more than a voluntary association for its structure, and it became incorporated as a membership corporation the year it moved.

Only six years later the deal with Mrs. Drexel came to an end and the club moved a second time to 238th Street and Broadway. It would have

This sketch of 1659 shows three men at court tennis, an indoor game, using a string instead of a net. Outside, others seem to be hitting a ball with rackets.

seemed that this was far enough to go to escape the march of residential progress, and from the fancy installation it looked in 1908 as though the West Side had found a permanent home. It covered two city blocks and had room for a dozen grass courts and fifteen clay courts around them. The pattern on which Forest Hills was later to be laid out had been established.

In the center of the property a substantial clubhouse in the style of summer cottages was put up. This two-story shingled building had a lounge and a porch with an awning where members could relax after their workouts. What put this setup far ahead of the original was the introduction of grass. Clay was more generally used throughout the country, but grass was the surface of championship events. The original motive of the first thirteen members to have a nice place to play tennis had been superceded by the ambition to have the best place in America to hold top tennis matches.

The move came at a time when tennis was in the doldrums, according to Parke Cummings, author of the history *American Tennis* (1957), and what put it there was Newport. Newport may have been right as the site of the national championships when the game began, but it had become a glaring anachronism in the twentieth century. Its rich patrons may have had great influence in the business world, but they came to Newport for a vacation, which meant sailing, golf and elaborate parties in their "cottages," vast summer palaces built for display. Their interest in tennis was on the level of their interest in opera. They could hum the tunes but they did not know the score.

The crowd at the Newport Casino came there not to watch tennis but to be seen. The nationals were as much a fashion show as a tennis tournament. Compared to Wimbledon, Newport was not a serious center of tennis. Many members of the West Side Tennis Club were dismayed by the atmosphere when they played in the championships or went up to watch them. Since many USLTA officials were West Side members, the grumbling represented a bid to move the nationals out of Newport and to New York's new grass courts. Here, at a serious tennis center, the crowds would be true tennis fans and not beautiful matrons showing off their huge hats and new egret feathers.

To prove this the club was invited in 1911 to stage the Davis Cup matches with Great Britain. This international competition had been conceived by Dwight Filley Davis of St. Louis in 1900, after he graduated from Harvard. He held the national doubles championships with Holcombe Ward and had completed a national tennis tour with some other players when he got the idea of inviting a British team to play an American team at Longwood, outside of Boston. The Longwood Cricket Club got its name from the estate at St. Helena where Napoleon lived in exile, but here the British team met its Waterloo and lost 3–0 to Ward and Davis in doubles and to Malcolm Whitman and Davis in singles. The American team was presented with a 13-inch-high sterling silver cup contributed by Davis, who had it made for him by the venerable Boston jewelers, Shreve, Crump & Low.

After three years of British–American play, Belgium and France entered the competition, and eventually the total number of nations playing rose to sixty-three. Prior to 1911, matches in America were played at the Crescent Athletic Club in Brooklyn and at the Germantown Cricket Club in Philadelphia. Public interest in international tennis was sufficient to bring 3,000 people a day to the wooden stands at the West Side courts. Three times as many people attended the Wimbledon fortnight, but the West Side's showing proved that good tennis could draw well in New York. And it was good tennis.

The American team consisted of William Larned, seven times national singles champion; Maurice McLoughlin, the first great player from California; Thomas Bundy, ranked third nationally; and Raymond D. Little, a member of the West Side. They beat the British 4–1. Little and Bundy lost the doubles to C. P. Dixon and A. E. Beamish, while Dixon and A. H. Lowe each lost their singles to McLoughlin and Larned. This was a zone match to determine which country would challenge the holder of the cup, Australasia (Australia and New Zealand were one country then). Later the Americans lost to Australasia in New Zealand.

The public fancied the most colorful player America had yet produced, Maurice McLoughlin, red-haired like Don Budge and called by the press the California Comet. Trained on the hard courts of the West, he had an overwhelming cannonball serve that allowed him to come to the net and dominate the play from that position. His was the first big game, and he played it three decades before another Californian, Jack Kramer, intro-

Lawn tennis, as it was enjoyed at the Toledo Outing Club in 1890.

38

Endorsement of tennis equipment by amateur champions raised no eyebrows in 1893. The wing collar assures readers of this newspaper ad that Oliver Campbell was a gentleman.

AUSTIN SMITH

A sketch of the West Side Tennis Club premises between 88th and 89th Streets on Central Park West in Manhattan. The shed at the left with five windows was the dressing room.

duced it as the definitive style of the post-World War II generation. Playing the grass-court circuit that had developed among the Eastern tennis clubs, McLoughlin proved that he could play well on any surface. He hit the ball harder than anyone heretofore, and the public loved him. But they had limited access to him, for there was no substantial arena in America where a real crowd could watch the national championships. In 1912 he won the national singles title at Newport, but he was indignant about the conditions of play. The noise may not have been as distracting as at a World Team Tennis match, but it was more annoying because it was the noise of inattention.

William Clothier, who had been singles champion in 1906, commented: "It is well known that the Newport gallery was at times noisy and not at all times concentrated on the play." And Maude Howe Elliott, daughter of Julia Ward Howe, wrote: "The beautiful women and their gay parasols served as a moving background that was trying for the players" (*This Was My Newport*, 1944).

Granted that Newport was inadequate, still the West Side Tennis Club could not really offer a more challenging alternative because it lacked the

39

space for a bigger crowd. Everyone was convinced by the outpouring of people for the Davis Cup that five times that number would pay to see great tennis in New York. But where would the club find the required terrain? Where the courts stood at 238th Street was the property of the Van Cortlandt Estate, and the club had a lease on it. One possibility was to buy the land and rearrange it to accommodate larger grandstands. Another was to move off Manhattan once and for all. Both possibilities were explored during the fall of 1911 and early 1912. The club had $13,000 available to buy a new site, and what determined them to leave 238th Street was the pressure from the Van Cortlandt Estate for immediate sale of the property. When the club hesitated, it was offered $12,000 to cancel the lease at once.

The hesitation occurred because the scope of the property did not seem quite big enough when compared to tracts outside the city that a committee had been looking over. By the end of the summer of 1912 the club had made up its collective mind to move somewhere. Just how Forest Hills became that somewhere is a story in itself.

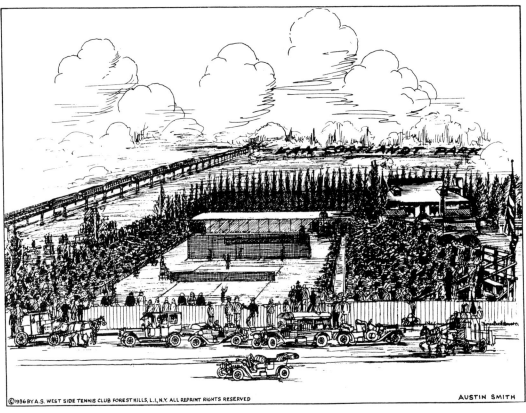

AUSTIN SMITH

40 *The West Side's spacious grounds near the northern boundary of the city at 238th Street and Broadway. The 1911 Davis Cup matches are in progress in this sketch. An ample clubhouse is among trees beyond the grandstand and, as at Forest Hills, a train is going by at left—the IRT subway, elevated in this region.*

3

$2,000 DOWN
AND A $75,000 MORTGAGE

THE COMMITTEE CHARGED WITH FINDING a suitable permanent home for the West Side Tennis Club—to be purchased, not rented—had considered parcels of land in the other four boroughs of New York (the Bronx, Queens, Brooklyn, Richmond—that is, Staten Island), as well as Nassau County, Long Island, and northern New Jersey. When a choice had been made after careful consideration of alternatives, it was agreed that the committee would present it to the entire club membership, which by then had risen to 600, and for this purpose a large meeting was held September 17, 1912, at the Hotel Manhattan. It did not go well.

With great gusto the chairman, Calhoun Craigin, described an ideal location suitable for holding the national championships someday. Craigin had been chairman of the Davis Cup committee in charge of those great matches a year before and was highly respected for that success. Now he spoke of a fantastic place, 10 acres that could be had for $72,000. It was located in Kew Gardens, a section of Queens.

The members did not share his enthusiasm, objecting to the location and the rail fare from the city, and so they appointed another committee, made up of five members, to seek offers from realtors up to the time of the annual meeting of the members on December 3. Within a month fifty-three offers came in, of which thirty were at once rejected. On October 16 the committee met with members again and reduced the properties under consideration to three: the Kew Gardens property, a parcel in the Bronx owned by Morris Park Estates and another at Forest Hills owned by the Sage Foundation Homes Company.

Edward C. Potter in his small volume *The West Side Tennis Club Story*, published by the club on its sixtieth anniversary, gives this account of what happened next:

> At the rather stormy meeting on December 3, two votes were taken. The first vote showed 186 in favor of Long Island and 126 in favor of the Bronx. A second vote showed a majority of approximately two to one in favor of the Forest Hills site as compared with Kew Gardens and a contract with the Sage Foundation Homes Company was therefore approved.

Thus the decision to move the club to Forest Hills was far from casual and was made only after very careful study and with the approval of a two-thirds majority of those voting. The responsibility for choosing Forest Hills rested in the end with the membership as a whole. The degree of participation in this crucial decision is impressive not only because of its democratic character but because it reveals a fundamental quality of the West Side membership, a willingness to work hard for the best interests of the club, to give up valuable time to promote the best in tennis. It was a persuasive factor that the USLTA found hard to resist in the long run, and of course the concern of many members for the well-being of the club persists to the present day.

Why Forest Hills? What was Forest Hills in 1912? Essentially a developer's vision. At this time the Borough of Queens, occupying as much land as Philadelphia and three times as much as Boston, was just beginning to be suburbanized and industrialized under such booster slogans as "The Borough of Magnificent Opportunities" and "The Fastest-Growing Borough of New York City." It was Queens that F. Scott Fitzgerald was wistfully recalling at the end of *The Great Gatsby:*

> . . . the old island here that flowered once for Dutch sailors' eyes —a fresh, green breast of the new world. . . . For an enchanted moment man must have held his breath in the presence of this continent, compelled into an aesthetic contemplation he neither understood nor desired, face to face for the last time in history with something commensurate to his capacity for wonder.

In 1609, Hendrick Hudson was the first white man to set foot on Queens, "a land of white sand, and a vast number of plum trees loaded with fruit, many covered with grape vines of different kinds," he wrote. Its produce was to help feed New York for centuries. Queens was counted as Dutch territory after Manhattan was purchased from Indians in 1623, but actual transfer of title did not occur until 1638, when the third Dutch

A new road for the benefit of buyers of lots in Forest Hills Gardens, a few years before the West Side moved out there.

At Station Square, lawns were put in while the scaffoldings on the inn and town houses were still up.

governor, Wilhelm Kieft, bought Queens from the Lenni-Lenape, an Algonquin tribe. The area of Forest Hills was called Whiteput by the Dutch, meaning a pit or hollow resulting from a dried stream bed. The British, in possession after 1664, changed it to Whitepot, and from that corruption came the legend that the land had been purchased from Indians for three white clay pots. In the seventeenth century there was a rural community of Whitepot belonging to the village of Newtown, founded by Englishmen in 1652. At first they called it Middleburgh after the capital of the province of Zealand in the Netherlands, where they had taken refuge as Puritans.

The Dutch of Long Island were not quite so hospitable as those in the homeland, and they refused to grant the settlers a patent for the Middleburgh land. Perhaps it was just a question of money, because the English then bought the land from local Indians in 1656. Once in possession, the English showed the limits of their own hospitality by restricting residence to those whom they considered desirable. You could only live in Middleburgh or Newtown if the community voted to accept you. Without knowing anything of this history, the planners of the modern community of Forest Hills Gardens imposed residency restrictions that did not lapse until recent years. It would not have been possible for just any group to have acquired the 10 acres the West Side Tennis Club got. So from its earliest days of occupation this ground had a very special character.

Newtown was in the county of Queens, a name taken in 1683 in honor

The 1911 Davis Cup matches at the West Side's 238th Street grounds. In the far court Maurice McLoughlin is returning the serve of Australia's Arthur Lowe, who lost in four sets to the California Comet.

Forest Hills was rolling farmland until the end of the nineteenth century.

of Charles II's wife, Catherine. Whitepot during the American Revolution was obliged to provision occupying British troops with grain, vegetables and meat, and the Americans could only travel to Manhattan with a pass. Among the 2,000 residents of Newtown in 1775 were 163 slaves. The land was by this time owned by a few families, and this persisted throughout the nineteenth century. Perhaps the largest land holding in Newtown belonged to Samuel Lord, founder of Lord & Taylor in New York City. He was an Englishman who fancied himself a country squire, and he built a mansion called Clermont Terrace. (By purest coincidence the estate in Bermuda where Mary Outerbridge first saw tennis was named Clermont.) Lord, however, preferred to live in England, so he left Clermont with his son-in-law, who sold it in 1893 to Cord Meyer, the first developer of this section of Queens, which is now known as Elmhurst.

It would be another generation before the development of Forest Hills became economically feasible. For Queens was underdeveloped by contrast with its neighbor, Brooklyn, the beneficiary of the Roeblings' magnificent Brooklyn Bridge, opened in 1883. Since the growth of Manhattan was northward, it made sense to link the crowded lower East Side to Brooklyn. The Queens crossing of the turbulent East River was by ferry—at 34th and 92nd Streets.

But by 1906 plans for the Queensboro Bridge linking Long Island City and mid-Manhattan were projected, and Cord Meyer that year bought 600 acres of farmland in the section of Whitepot called Hopedale. This choice property abutted the public Forest Park, so Meyer called his project

Forest Hills, though the highest point above mean water there is only 160 feet. In fact the land is not exactly flat and does roll slightly, but anyone looking from the top of West Side Stadium today would be hard put to point out any substantial changes in elevation. But the word *hills* has a nice residential character, so prospective buyers of homes would be considering a good address with none of the real disadvantages of hills, such as getting up the icy roads in winter, or getting the runoff of water from your neighbor on high.

Even more important than the Queensboro Bridge for cars and wagons was the promised Long Island Railroad Tunnel that would put Forest Hills only a quarter of an hour from Manhattan by electrified train. This was actually opened September 10, 1910. But meanwhile land sales had languished because the only public transportation from Forest Hills was a bus to Elmhurst operated by the Cord Meyer Development Company. There were already sixty-four residential sections in Queens competing with one another for new home owners. "Here is where the future millions of New York City's ever-increasing population will be housed," the Queens Chamber of Commerce proclaimed. But Cord Meyer could not be sure that his particular tracts of land would be taken up quickly now, so he offered to sell a large block of his holdings, 142 acres, to the Sage Foundation Homes Company in 1908. There could not have been a better buyer for this property.

Sage Foundation Homes was a subsidiary of the Russell Sage Foundation, a philanthropic institution run by the widow of one of the great financial operators of the nineteenth century. Mrs. Sage was in ways as unusual as her husband, an upstate New York wholesale grocer whom she married when she was already a forty-one-year-old schoolteacher with high ideals. As Russell Sage moved out of the grocery business and into politics and eventually into railroad stock speculation, Margaret Olivia Slocum Sage held their style of living to modest proportions and laid plans for substantial philanthropies. During the last five years of Sage's life she ran his business affairs with great shrewdness, and after he died in 1906 she set up the foundation bearing his name with a $10 million fund. The purpose was the improvement of social and living conditions, and one of its projects was to build low-cost houses. This latter objective was to be confusing when Forest Hills Gardens was created.

Over the years the Russell Sage Foundation has distributed $30 million in grants to eighteen colleges, including the women's college in Troy bearing Sage's name, as well as to the American Museum of Natural History and the Metropolitan Museum of Art. How then did a charitable foundation come to devote time and money to the creation of one of the most elegant residential sections in the entire city of New York? It was simply a real estate investment. In those days foundations were more likely to put their capital into land than into stocks or bonds.

This particular land provided an opportunity for Sage to be a pacesetter in suburban development by creating the finest residential section

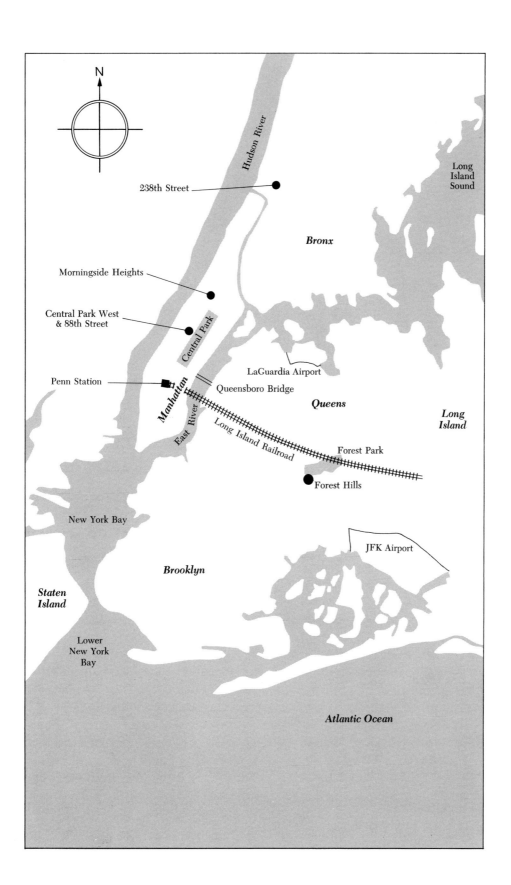

N

238th Street

Hudson River

Long
Island
Sound

Bronx

Morningside Heights

Central Park West
& 88th Street

Central Park

Penn Station

Manhattan

LaGuardia Airport

Queensboro Bridge

Queens

Long
Island

East River

Long Island Railroad

Forest Park

Forest Hills

New York Bay

JFK Airport

Brooklyn

Staten
Island

Lower
New York
Bay

Atlantic Ocean

Across the Fields, Forest Hills, N. Y.

The home of Samuel Lord, founder of Lord & Taylor, who was one of the early residents.

View of the Station, Forest Hills, N. Y.

The Long Island Railroad station at Forest Hills.

ever built in New York at one time. The proceeds, of course, would be donated to education and art. But the aim of the foundation in being the *best* in housing was quite clear, and it coincided with the West Side Tennis Club's determination to be the best in tennis.

The company's objectives were set forth in a pamphlet entitled "A Forward Movement in Suburban Development." It called for consideration of the community as a whole, with "a definite architectural treatment of the houses and buildings so that when the whole is completed there will be harmony and not strife in the close relation which each house must necessarily bear to its neighbors." The concept has an ironic ring in view of recent developments in the area, which took the form of bitter protest against substantial interracial low-cost housing. Like the Founding Fathers of the Republic, the Sage management tried to protect its creation against future pressures for change. It drew up "carefully thought restrictions designed to protect the investor and to maintain his home in surroundings, the character of which will not be subject to radical changes." As a result the section looks today much as it did three generations ago.

Everything the Sage group did was first class. Frederick Law Olmstead, the greatest landscape architect in American history, was responsible for laying out a boulevard and a main street, between which ran curving, narrow residential streets that would not support heavy traffic. The "cozy

Queens Boulevard, Forest Hills, N. Y.

At the time the West Side Tennis Club moved to Forest Hills, Queens Boulevard had a country-town look.

50   *After the first great Davis Cup matches at Forest Hills in 1914, the formally attired crowd crossed a clay court on the way to the Long Island Railroad depot, which was directly connected to the old Forest Hills Inn. The vacant lot is now occupied by an apartment house. The tracks are above Burns Street, and the corner is Tennis Place.*

domestic character" was enhanced by common areas of 1½ and 3½ acres, two parks of 1 and 1½ acres, and private sections, open only to the back gates of the residents, where children could play together unthreatened by the outside world.

The developers stated: "They have thought that homes could be supplied like those in garden cities of England." In one instance the houses were row houses, but the rest were to stand alone, looking much alike, with stucco and half-timbering in the neo-Tudor style of the day dominating what the developers called "a homogeneous and congenial community."

Since the railroad was the key to the development, the first place the prospective buyer arriving from the city would see was of critical importance. So the developers concentrated their attention on the depot and its surroundings. The railroad had $10,000 to put into a conventional building, but the Sage Foundation said it would contribute $20,000 for something unusual, and Cord Meyer agreed to do likewise. For $50,000 a highly attractive building with a double staircase in stone was built to harmonize with a picturesque inn constructed across what was called Station Square by Grosvenor Atterbury, the chief architect for the development. The railroad agreed to name this stop not just Forest Hills but Forest Hills Gardens, the name of the Sage development.

When the committee from the West Side Tennis Club marched down the station steps, walked across the cobbled square where cab horses stood at a stone trough, looked at the red-tile roof of the gracious inn with its unusual tower and covered bridge connection to the station platform, and then saw that they could have 10 acres only a block from this spot, they were hooked. They knew instantly how easy it would be to draw a crowd of tennis enthusiasts from the city to see the big matches. And they were so right!

The marvel of it all was that it was only a fourteen-minute ride to Penn Station in midtown. "The ride," said the reassuring brochure, "is an agreeable one, consisting of four minutes through a cool, well-ventilated tunnel and about ten minutes through pleasant open country." The fare was 45 cents one way and $6.80 a month for a commutation ticket.

There were restrictions at Forest Hills Gardens prohibiting any "brewery, distillery, malt house, slaughter house, brass foundry, tin, nail or other iron foundry, lime kiln or sugar bakery, tallow chandler, hospital, asylum or institution of kindred nature, stable of any kind (except on designated lots)." Other prohibited manufacturers were vitreol, cream of tartar and dynamite.

The terms of purchase for home owners then seem reasonable enough today. Lots could be bought for 2 percent cash and ten years to pay at 4½ percent interest. There was no concealing the intent to make a profit, but the developers held that "a distinct educational purpose exists," namely, "the need of better and more attractive housing facilities in the suburbs for persons of modest means who could pay from $25 a month upward in the purchase of a home." Then came a curious exposure of social conscience that harks back to that low-cost housing project Mrs. Sage had in mind:

"Some people may ask why the first housing plan of the Sage Foundation does not provide for the laboring man, whose wages are small. The Sage Foundation has not forgotten the laboring man. It may be able to announce something for his benefit later on, but the cost of the land at Forest Hills Gardens and the character of its surroundings preclude provision there for the day laborer."

And provision for others, too, was precluded by gentlemen's agreements. Forest Hills Gardens was very much white, Anglo-Saxon and Protestant, as were many surburban developments, at a time when the waves of immigrants from southern and eastern Europe were still pouring into the country through Ellis Island. It is a sensitive issue even today. Those who live in the environs of Forest Hills Gardens are quick to tell strangers that the Gardens are no longer restricted.

To have the country's finest tennis club at Forest Hills with the promise of national publicity for its big matches and crowds of people who had never been to Queens before was all a welcome prospect to Sage Foundation Homes. The price of the little more than 10 acres was $77,000, and it called for a down payment of $2,000 in cash. A 5 percent mortgage for $75,000 was obtained, and plans were drawn for a clubhouse to cost $25,000. This investment was predicated on the sound anticipation of considerable revenue from the gate receipts of the Davis Cup and, it was hoped, of national championship matches.

Arrangements were completed in the winter of 1913, when the club still retained its property at 238th Street in the city. The spring and summer months saw a gradual transition to the new location, and Calhoun Craigin supervised the transfer of the best turf at 238th Street to a location in front of the future clubhouse at Forest Hills. This was done only after the 1913 Davis Cup matches were played in upper Manhattan before another overflow crowd, who saw McLoughlin, R. Norris Williams and Harold H. Hackett beat the Australasian team of Stanley Doust, Horace Rice and A. B. Jones by 4–1, losing only the doubles. Eighteen new turf courts were seeded for play in 1914, while by the fall of 1913 twenty-one clay courts on the periphery of the turf were already playable, and fifteen more were to be added by spring, when the clubhouse would be open. So in little more than a year's time everything at the West Side Tennis Club you see today was in place except for the Stadium and Grandstand.

The grounds committee reported in January 1914: "We believe that the Club has now the best turf and clay courts it has ever had and that they are equal to any in the world." In fact the entire arrangement of a field of turf bound by clay, all of which was visible from the clubhouse, provided a setting second only to Wimbledon.

It was time for a wider world to know more about this new place called Forest Hills.

4

THE GREATEST
DAVIS CUP MATCH

THE STAGE WAS NOW SET. Tennis had its potential theater. But like some theaters of Greek antiquity—at Delphi, for instance—it would be necessary for the spectators to travel from the city to the arena. The idea of tennis being a form of theater may seem farfetched, for theater has had either religious, political or social significance that seems to be utterly lacking in tennis, a mere game, a diversion, an exercise, a test of excellence, and more recently a commercial undertaking like a Broadway play. However, the use of the word *play* in both theater and tennis or any sport using a ball or puck (you do not "play" track or swimming) is suggestive of a link between the two activities. For the big tournaments, Forest Hills even has "producers."

Just why the West Side Tennis Club set out as a matter of deliberate policy to turn its grounds into what came to be called the shrine of American tennis has never been explained except in the banal terms of modern psychology—drive for power, outlet for ambitions frustrated elsewhere, hunger for reflected glory and so on. Such motivation is seen to be rooted in some evil force lurking only in certain circles, the wealthy and powerful.

Another view might be that tennis is a form of celebration of life at its most challenging level. Its rapid evolution from a casual, light-hearted exchange at teatime to a grim struggle engaging the whole body and soul may simply disclose man's eternal response to the possibilities his body and mind and spirit can accomplish. It is not enough to test these possibilities alone. Witnesses are required to validate whatever claims the players make, and like the original attendants of Dionysian festivals, the crowd participates actively and not passively in the ceremony. "Even the most experienced athlete," Don Budge has observed, "plays better when he is appreciated."

It is now commonplace to say that all the staging of pro tennis can ultimately be justified in terms of the health of the nation because it encourages more people to take up the game and to exercise. At Forest Hills in 1914 no one yet felt it necessary to sanctify the club's purposes by claims invoking the national interest. It was only when the United States went to war that tennis was discovered to be essential to America's health.

It was the Davis Cup play that the club had its eyes on. It was to be the set piece that would establish Forest Hills' primacy in American tennis. But international goodwill arising from the Davis Cup became insignificant when the Austrian Archduke Franz Ferdinand was assassinated at Sarajevo on June 28, and war began on July 3 between Austria and Serbia. Germany had already been at war with the Allies almost a month when the time came for the Davis Cup challenge round between the holder of the cup, the United States, and the winner of the international-zone tournament, Australasia. As in earlier national tournaments, the champion or cup holder was not obliged to "play through" half a dozen matches but could grandly sit it out until a challenger emerged and then play a final or challenge round. This practice was not eliminated in the Davis Cup until 1972, and now the cup holder enters the draw from the beginning. Having twice staged Davis Cup matches in New York, the West Side again sought from the USLTA and obtained that right in 1914.

The three consecutive days of play were scheduled for August 13, 14 and 15. Happily for Forest Hills there was no suggestion that the matches be canceled because of the British Empire's mobilization. Large wooden grandstands like those that had served at 238th Street but much vaster—forty rows high—were set up in front of the clubhouse parallel to the Long Island Railroad tracks a few dozen yards behind the north stands. In front of the clubhouse itself there were box seats and rows of chairs for members under very broad, striped awnings. The club members had access to cold drinks at a bar, but with more than a thousand people on the actual clubhouse premises it was a lottery as to who got served. Actually the weather was perfect that first day, with the temperature at 76 and humidity only 46 percent.

The clubhouse was what it is today with the exception of space later added to the second floor by building atop a terrace and cutting off a graceful roof line. It is a two-story domestic Tudor structure, stucco and half-timber, stark from without and rather bare within, architecturally unoriginal but not lacking in charm and attractiveness. It could hardly be called imposing, yet because it sits alone at the head of a field of brilliant emerald grass it has the appearance of a headquarters of tennis. The venue is so attractive that on the opening day in 1914 it instantly won the affection of the 12,000 people who overflowed the stands. It was the largest crowd ever to watch tennis. This crowd, incidentally, is not much smaller than today's daily gatherings for the Open. When the Stadium was built in 1923 the capacity was set at 14,000 or slightly less.

Although this crowd faithfully turned up three days running, it was the first day's match between the Australian Norman E. Brookes and the California Comet, McLoughlin, that was most talked about. It is considered one of the most dramatic of all tennis matches and possibly the greatest Davis Cup singles ever played. The popular response to this one match was undoubtedly the clinching argument for removing the national championships from remote Newport and putting them in the most populous city in the country.

The American team of Maurice McLoughlin, R. Norris Williams and T. C. Bundy provided just about the best players in the country. McLoughlin had been ranked number one for the last two years and Williams number two. Williams was ranked one two years later. Bundy had ranked two in 1911 but was unranked in 1914, yet he was a strong doubles player because of his masterful twist serve. In Norman Brookes the Australasians had a folk hero who had made his first appearance at Wimbledon in 1905, was Wimbledon champion in 1907 and again when he returned to England in 1914. In the age of steamships, travel between England and Australia was not undertaken lightly. Brookes's teammate was a popular young player, Anthony Wilding of New Zealand, who was expected eventually to supersede Brookes as the champion of Australasia (he died in the war in 1915).

On opening day Wilding played the first match against Williams and won in straight sets. Then, at about 3:15, McLoughlin and Brookes began to warm up. What a study in contrasts. The American was twenty-four and his opponent thirty-seven! You could tell from their clothes that there was a generation gap. Brookes wore a gray cloth cap, a long-sleeved white shirt and white buck shoes. Red-haired McLoughlin had no cap, wore a short-sleeved white shirt and black calf shoes. Both men wore long white flannel trousers with cuffs. Their shoes each had a dozen ¼-inch steel spikes.

McLoughlin was familiar to New Yorkers from his earlier Davis Cup match. Brookes was a legend. The son of a self-made British immigrant to Australia, he had been able to devote much of his adult life to tennis and to being a celebrity. His wedding in London in 1911 attracted such crowds that police barriers were needed. The wedding cake befitted the world's greatest tennis player—it was decorated with silver rackets, nets and tennis balls. Though he was getting old for match play and suffered from chronic stomach ulcers, he was famous for his stubbornness and he hated to be beaten. Tilden, Gonzales, Rosewall exemplified the Brookes spirit as they grew older.

But McLoughlin was a formidable opponent trained on the hard courts of California, where, as he himself described it, "the fast-bounding

55

ball meets the player." As a result, he had learned to go for the kill quicker than Eastern grass-court players, who he said played "a strokier game" and had better ground strokes than Western players. Brookes, who played mostly on grass, was in this sense an "Eastern" player, and was stronger from the baseline than McLoughlin. This distinction today can be made between men and women on grass or between men on grass and men on clay. Only the greatest players play equally well on all surfaces—Laver is an example. Borg is weaker on grass than on clay.

The Aussies came to Forest Hills after thoroughly trouncing the German Davis Cup team at Pittsburgh 5–0. Australasia, as part of the British Empire, was on the brink of war with Germany, and the Germans said they would leave the court if war was declared. On the last day of the challenge rounds at Pittsburgh, August 1, war did break out, but officials took great care to conceal the news until after the matches. The Aussies were remembered for beating the United States 5–0 in New Zealand in 1911, when Brookes beat McLoughlin in five sets and the American champion William Larned went down in four to Rodney Heath. The crowd yearned for an American win, especially after Williams's dispirited loss to Wilding.

In the first set it was for a long while impossible to tell any difference between Brookes and McLoughlin, as there was no service break. Brookes, a left-hander, perhaps the greatest lefty until Laver, consistently followed his serve into the net and so did McLoughlin. Then at 8–9 Brookes seemed to solve the Californian's serve and put away three quick returns with sharp wrist strokes to make it love–40, set point.

McLoughlin had been using a twist serve. "In match play I never use a great variety of services. It is quality that counts and placing," he wrote in *Tennis as I Play It* (1915).

But what is a *great* variety? With three set points facing him, he switched to a flat serve and got to deuce. Then came a twist followed by a winning chop volley. He took the game with a blazing ace. "I certainly wish never to be subjected to that strain again," he commented.

The service duel went to 15–all. The scoreboard ran out of numerals. The crowd was numb with tension. Brookes was later described in the press as "saturnine and grim," while McLoughlin, who smiled a lot, had "a winning personality." The redhead's racket was compared with "the club of a primitive caveman" on overhead shots that brought roars from the crowd. The American was not all smash (McLoughlin's quaint phrase for the smash was "down stroke"); he had a concealed lob which started out looking like a deep forehand passing shot.

But the spectacular leaping smash was what lingered in the memory of sportswriter Al Laney of the New York *Herald Tribune* years later. He describes a picture of "McLoughlin, all fire and dash, leaping from the ground to smash a lob and, as the ball bit into the turf and bounded impossibly away, of Brookes dropping his racket, raising both hands above his head in despair and calling on high heaven to witness his misfortune. This happened several times near the end of that tense set."

McLoughlin finally outplayed the older man by brainy maneuvering.

Dwight Davis stands behind the sterling cup he donated. Malcolm Whitman, left, and Holcombe Ward were the others members of the first Davis Cup team. Notice the high, spiked shoes.

Norman Brookes, in his familiar cloth cap, was Australia's great hope in the 1914 Davis Cup matches at Forest Hills.

He won 17–15, "a triumph of brains rather than one of mechanical strokes," said *American Lawn Tennis* magazine. A. Wallis Myers, the London writer, commented that the set had "never been exceeded for speed of stroke and sustained aggression on both sides." McLoughlin had twelve aces in the first set to Brookes's seven, but Brookes hit fifteen winning returns of serve to McLoughlin's three.

McLoughlin finished the match in straight sets, 6–3, 6–3, a total of fifty games in two hours (by no means a record). Davis Cup matches are still played without resort to the tie breaker, which was introduced to satisfy time limitations imposed by tournaments and by TV. Ashe took eighty-six games to beat Kuhnke in America's 5–0 defeat of Germany at Cleveland in 1970. There is something to be said for long matches—occasionally.

Wilding lost to McLoughlin in four sets in 1914 the next day, and then teamed with Brookes in the doubles and beat McLoughlin and Bundy to take the cup. That was the end of international play until 1919, after the

Ten minutes to four, August 13, 1914. In the third set, America's Thomas C. Bundy, using a Western grip, volleys toward Australia's Anthony Wilding. McLoughlin watches while Brookes, in the cap, moves in.

Practicing for the first big matches started in 1914 at Forest Hills. Maurice McLoughlin in the far court moves in on a shot from R. Norris Williams, his Davis Cup teammate.

This picture of the West Side's layout was probably taken in the early twenties, judging from the growth of ivy on the clubhouse. The spaces on either side of the front courts were once clay courts, sacrificed to the building of grandstands.

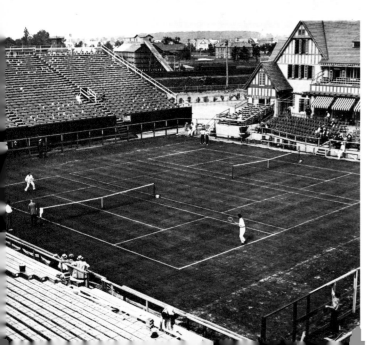

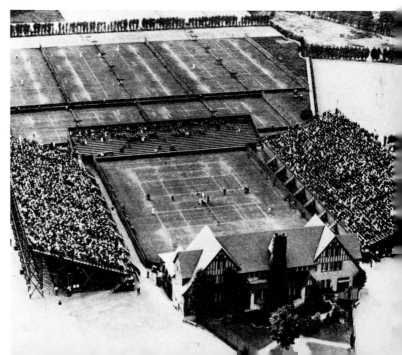

Armistice of 1918 ended the First World War. But it was the beginning of Forest Hills as the major American tennis center.

Although occupying only a fourth of the acreage of Wimbledon, it won instant distinction and admiration from British sportswriters. A. Wallis Myers spotted the difference between an American and a British tennis crowd in his report on the Davis Cup in *Ayres Lawn Tennis Almanack* for 1915:

> Those who would criticize the bearing of an American crowd must remember that America has no leisured class, no floating community which can take a sequestered draught of games as our old gentlemen do at Lords! Virtually every man and a large percentage of the women assembled round the court in New York had been at business in the morning. They brought their keen brains from the desk and the store into the stands. Theirs was no perfunctory interest, no hour idly spent in pursuit of some new pleasure. Thus an American crowd—an American city crowd I should add—like to see a match pursued with the honest noise and exacting speed of their business hours and their railways. And yet leavening this somewhat rough demeanor is a sense of justice and fair play. The American has no time for bullying.

This topic of the crowd at Forest Hills is important. The crowd at Newport had a different character. Not coming from the desk and the store but from the mansion, the links, the yacht or the beach, it was a resort crowd attending matches more because it was the *in* thing to do at the time. McLoughlin in particular was annoyed at the inattention of the spectators, whose chattering distracted him. He was too much of a gentleman to commit his annoyance to print, but he could pay tribute to Forest Hills, and he wrote:

> Three consecutive days this huge throng assembled over twelve thousand each day, and the behavior and sportsmanlike demeanor of this great mass of people left nothing to be desired. They were wonderfully restrained when the occasion demanded and equally so were they responsive at other times.

They looked more like a city crowd, many men in somber business suits and most wearing straw hats (it was a predominantly male crowd).

So although America lost the Davis Cup and was not to recover it until the next time it formed a team—in 1920—it gained the ideal terrain for championship tennis. Oddly, the defeat of Brookes was McLoughlin's peak performance, and thereafter he declined rapidly, losing at Newport to Williams in the national finals later in August, and the following year at Forest Hills to the new sensation, William M. Johnston. Something happened to the serve of the California Comet, who flashed across the horizons of international tennis a brief seven years and then withdrew from the scene. Allison Danzig, the dean of tennis reporters, wrote: "That match [against Brookes] and the fancy that the public took to McLoughlin had much to do with popularizing lawn tennis. The California Comet's spectacular style of play opened the eyes of the uninitiated to the fact that tennis was a vigorous sport and a stern test of physical fitness."

Of this test Tilden once said: "Tennis puts an athlete under the hardest physical, mental and nervous strain of any game played by mankind." Joe Hunt, the 1943 titleholder, played football at Annapolis but considered tennis a tougher sport.

Brookes never really left the tennis world until he was an old man. He continued to play tournaments until he was almost fifty, and he nearly beat Tilden at close to this age. He ran his country's lawn tennis federation and captained the Australian Davis Cup team as late as 1935. He was knighted in 1939. "The Mighty Brookes" became Sir Norman, a distinguished businessman and outspoken force for amateur tennis (he could not abide professionalism, but then he was a rich man and needed no money from the game).

And so the year 1914 ended with America isolated by the European war, which put an end to tennis tournaments abroad. But there would be the American national championships in 1915 and the question of the moment became: Would they be played at frothy Newport or would they be shifted to Forest Hills?

Maurice McLoughlin, using the Western grip, at Forest Hills' inaugural Davis Cup matches in 1914.

Mary K. Browne, left, and Molla Bjurstedt Mallory in 1924.

60

5

NEWPORT LOSES THE NATIONALS

So far Newport has been mentioned only as it was seen during the last years the national championships were held there, when it had become outdated by the development of tennis as a sport of great national and international importance. It is always easy to be critical of an *ancien régime* representative of a small exclusive upper class. But to Newport American tennis owes a very great deal. However superficially interested the Newport crowd was in watching tennis, the fact remains that the Newport Casino gave the national championships a cachet no other place could have.

At this beautiful, picturesque and quite unique club the USLTA was putting tennis on display for a highly influential group that would support the game, encourage it in their children and see to its development in the schools and colleges they attended. Tennis needed this private support because it was not forthcoming from public sources—and still is not. It is worth noting that even today in the Soviet Union, which has great international players like Metreveli and Morozova, there is little support for tennis. "In Moscow most courts belong to private sports clubs sponsored by government ministries and agencies," *The New York Times* reported on October 16, 1974.

In one way Newport had and still has more to offer than Forest Hills;

it is a seaside resort with an ambiance of comfort and gaiety that Queens does certainly not have. Many players stayed in luxury, in delightful summer homes. They attended parties and dances, where they were the center of attention. In the prewar days Forest Hills had a bit of this at the inn, where dances were held and players could take rooms or in a few homes in the Gardens. But the charms of Newport are unique.

In the eighteenth century Newport was a more promotional commercial port than New York and was already attracting summer visitors from the South and the West Indies. The northern capital of the slave trade, it declined sharply after the American Revolution and quite deliberately determined that its future rested on exploiting its beaches and waters as an exclusive summer resort. Much like Queens, Newport was developed by turning open land into house lots, beginning in 1845, when 300 acres were laid out in new streets and plots. In 1857 a promotional reunion of former residents, called Exiles from Eden, drew hundreds of visitors, many of whom became regular summer cottagers. The Southern clientele was replaced by a few enormously rich Northern families like the Astors, Vanderbilts, Belmonts and others with money enough to follow them, and the fortunes made after the Civil War allowed a kind of conspicuous and lavish entertainment unknown to that quiet town. Fashionable picnics and elaborate rustic dances in barns gave way to cotillions and yacht club parties.

For a time an entire beach, Bailey's Beach, was preempted for the exclusive use of "society," leaving the hostile natives and common visitors to bathe elsewhere. When the herd gradually encroached on this strand, society withdrew.

"Pavillons that recall Coney Island more than old Newport have arisen," one observer wrote, "and an aroma of chowder pervades them." He also noted that "the future of Newport is, one must admit, considerably complicated by the peril of snobbishness."

But there was a sporting side to Newport. It was a yachting center. There were horse shows. The same year the national tennis championships began there, 1881, the Newport Skating Rink (roller skating) opened. The country's first international polo match was held in Newport in 1886 and the first National Open Golf Championship took place at the Newport Country Club in 1895. All of nineteen cars turned out in the nation's first horseless carriage parade there in 1899, cars nicknamed by their mistresses Puff-puff, Angelica and Toby, symbolic of the matriarchy that governed the town's social life.

Tennis was a natural for the grassy estates, and they first appeared in Newport in 1875. When James Gordon Bennett ordered the noted architectural firm of McKim, Mead and White to build a club opposite his home on Bellevue Avenue in 1880, he did not conceive of it as exclusively devoted to tennis, a game he seldom played. Shortly after its completion Bennett turned the Casino over to a membership corporation and withdrew from the scene.

Casino lawns were surrounded by walks, and members gathered there, much as the English upper classes did at eighteenth-century Bath, to stroll around the quadrangle of low, shingled buildings with a modest clock tower at one end and a graceful piazza at the other. Weekly concerts and dances were well attended. Today you can still dine on the porch of a moderately priced restaurant facing the quadrangle.

Despite the atmosphere of a lawn party, the national championships saw the development of the first great American player, Richard Sears of Boston, the game's earliest volleyer, who began playing with a court-tennis curved racket, later discarded for a mammoth 16-ounce straight racket. Sears, wearing steel-rimmed glasses, striped blazer, necktie and cricket cap, was still not too encumbered to introduce the lob and the overhand serve, and for seven years he held the championship, a record never surpassed, and equaled among the men only by Larned and Tilden. Although he never got beyond the first round at Wimbledon, he returned from England with the Lawford stroke, employing a Western grip to impart top spin.

It became the custom to give the winner's trophy permanently to anyone who won three championships. After Sears, O. S. Campbell, Malcolm Whitman and William Larned each retired cups won at Newport. Only once did a foreigner win there—Laurie Doherty of England, in 1903.

A travel book of the day gives this description of the nationals at Newport:

> There are probably few prettier scenes than that of which this contest is the centre. Perfectly trimmed lawns swept by the freshest and daintiest morning dresses, young men in flannels, rosy with health and irresponsibility, fashion in its freest and least conscious manifestations, the mass of "best people" in their most attractive inadvertence, the rising seats around the courts clad in the most refreshing variety of clear-colored costumes pieced out with patches of brilliant parasols, the watercolor note everywhere, as a painter would say, and the well-groomed young fellows in the centre of the composition obviously exhibiting both strength and skill—make a picture which for combined animation and refinement, both of actors and spectators, it would be difficult to match anywhere.

Somewhere in this picture there is a tennis match going on, but without much sweat. It was the custom of the summer millionaires to refer to those local townsmen who provisioned them and worked for them as their "footstools." In a sense the tennis players were decorative footstools who came for a week to add a new diversion for the easily bored elegant people.

Yet the Casino was well managed and did not stand still by any means. In 1914 the club acquired another 10 acres to expand the court area and spent $50,000 on improvements in order to make the 1915 nationals a bigger success than ever. No doubt the threat posed by Forest Hills stimulated this investment. As early as 1911 there was talk about finding another site, and players, especially those from the hard-court West, were openly critical of the atmosphere.

Fans were not lacking. Perhaps 4,000 to 5,000 attended the finals in 1914, coming by train from Boston, Providence and New York (you could also come by boat) and locally by auto. But the traffic congestion was awful. There was no hotel in town, not one, so visitors paid outrageous prices for rooms in eighteenth-century houses that were not very comfortable. It all seemed so inadequate and inappropriate to an event of such national importance. Newport was fashionable but provincial.

By 1914 Woodrow Wilson's New Freedom meant a federal income tax, and Henry Ford's assembly line paid $5 a day to men working a mere forty-hour week. The gap between class and mass was closing ever so slightly, and Newport represented a kind of atmosphere of exclusiveness that was on the wane. The death of J. P. Morgan in 1913 seemed to come at the right time.

During the autumn of 1914 certain West Side members began lobbying with USLTA officials to get the nationals away from Newport the next year. Foremost among the lobbyists was the dynamic Julian Myrick, who eventually became the president of the USLTA and of the West Side Tennis Club. The pressure for holding the championships was unofficial, for there were some West Side members who had no desire to clutter up their club with such an undertaking. At this time no other club was putting itself forward as a successor to Newport, and Newport confidently expected that its expenditure for new courts, together with thirty-three years of tradition, would be sufficient insurance to head off the aggressive New York crowd's not very subtle maneuvering. In fact there was little Newport could do until open hostilities actually occurred. These took the form of a Players' Committee, organized for the specific purpose of shifting the championship matches to New York. Whether or not this was the brainchild of Myrick no one will ever know. It does seem somewhat disingenuous of the club to have announced publicly on January 9, 1915, after its annual meeting that it was not striving to get the nationals away from Newport.

There was a conflict of interest, according to press reports, inasmuch as some of the members of the Players' Committee belonged to the West Side. And three members of the club identified themselves as opposed to holding the All Comers, as the tournament was called, on their new courts —D. Little, Dean Mathey and Louis Graves.

The Players' Committee of about a hundred had some important people in it, including Dwight Davis, father of the Davis Cup, Holcombe Ward, Karl Behr, J. R. Strachan and C. J. Griffin, all ranked in the top ten at one time or another. Its secretary was Lyle Mahan of the West Side Tennis Club! On Sunday, January 17, three weeks before the annual meeting of the USLTA, the players served a cannonball in the form of a letter calling for removal of the championships from Newport to New York. "WEST SIDE MAY GET NATIONALS AWAY FROM NEWPORT," ran the banner on the sports section of *The New York Times*. The letter advised the USLTA: "Tennis is no longer the pastime of a few but has come to be a national heritage." The players argued from a position of power. New York, they held, was the center of American tennis, with fifty-eight of the top one hundred ranking players. Half of the 260 clubs in the USLTA were located in metropolitan New York.

The ensuing debate in the press had a who-struck-John quality, with accusations followed by counteraccusations. Newport's defenders were led by Charles M. Bull of Brooklyn's Crescent Athletic Club, and he was supported by the national champion, Dick Williams. They ridiculed the West Side's pretensions. The Players' Committee retorted that they were only concerned about the "good of the game." Newport said there would be an embarrassing surplus of entrants in New York, for the All Comers meant just that: anyone could enter the tournament. But who was going to journey to remote Newport except qualified players? The implication was that in New York every hacker who ever got a first serve in would want to play. Well, said the Players, the West Side has twice as many courts as Newport. Furthermore, "Tennis outgrew Newport a number of years ago, but Boston's grasp on the game has been until now too hard to break. Tennis may formerly have belonged as it did to that section of the country, but who will now assert that it has not outgrown Boston?" Here were the makings of a civil war.

Fair play was called for by Newport in view of the enormous outlay for new courts made by the Casino in anticipation of the nationals. It would not be right to take away the tournament on such short notice. Nonsense, was the retort, those courts were built for the expanded membership to play on. All of this was carried on in the press. There was bickering about misrepresentation after the Players said that only a few hundred spectators attended the finals at Newport in 1914. Bull pointed out correctly that there were thousands there. Yes, answered the Players, but only a few hundred played tennis! "Unless a man plays a game he is unlikely to be an enthusiast." It was the hope of the Players to fill the stands almost exclusively with New York tennis players. This seemed like the weakest of arguments, as if the crowds at the Harvard–Yale game were made up of halfbacks and tackles. But there was something about the quality of the spectators at Newport that truly rankled those on the courts.

The lack of screens behind the baseline impaired visibility of the ball. "It is unfair to say some courts have no background but moving people," Bull wrote, and pointed out that there were screens; but in fact they were only 3 feet high. And people did move about a lot, as they still do at Forest Hills and Wimbledon; but the motive for this, the Players said, was "as much to see the latest frocks and dresses as the latest tennis played." Maude Howe Elliott, the Newport denizen, conceded this in her memoirs: "In fact Newport's whole attitude towards tennis was social rather than sporting. So in the end we lost the national tournaments."

An argument advanced against Newport was its lack of hotel facilities,

65

At the Newport Casino in 1891, F. H. Hovey, left, is playing M. D. Smith in the semifinals of the national championships.

Bill Larned, seven times national singles champion at Newport between 1901 and 1911.

The Newport Casino, where the National Lawn Tennis Hall of Fame and Tennis Museum is housed.

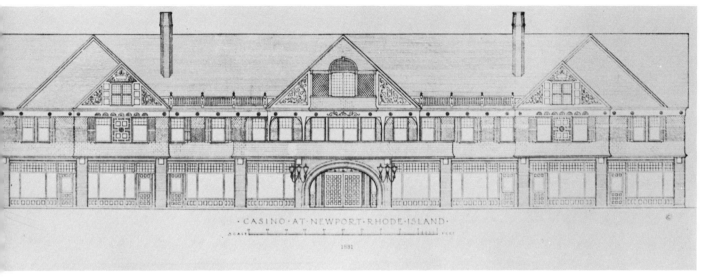

Architects'—McKim, Mead and White—rendering of the Newport Casino.

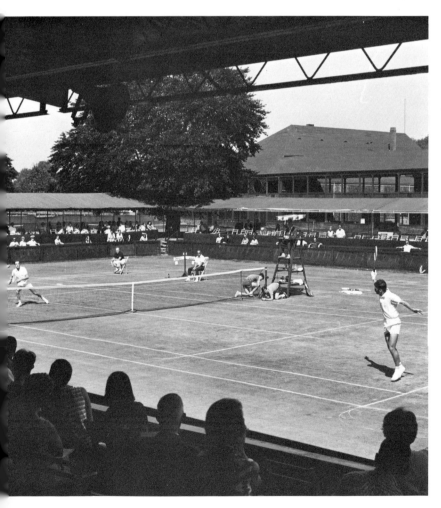

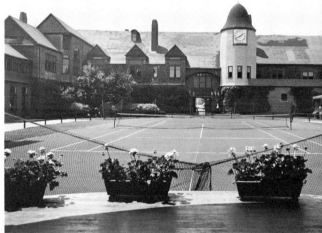

The inner court of the Newport Casino, originally a tea garden, contains the only hard-surface court on the grounds. The Tennis Hall of Fame Museum is at the left.

Newport is still a great tennis center, one of the few remaining places where tournaments will be played on grass. The players are Okker (at net) and Riessen.

The crowd at the national championships in 1906 (shot in three exposures). Note that the women outnumber the men.

and this was indisputable, although Bull could claim that the rates for accommodations were comparable with those in New York. But you paid about as much for a domestic bedroom with cold water in a pitcher in Newport as for a hotel room and bath in Manhattan.

Bull was not winning the argument, so he abandoned the debate and tried action. On January 23 the clubs of Philadelphia, speaking through A. L. Hopkins of the Merion Cricket Club, vowed to keep the tournament at Newport. Hopkins was a vice-president of the deciding body, the USLTA, so here was another instance of advocacy by one of the judges. Hopkins attacked the commercialism of sports in New York.

"The West Side Tennis Club is merely a landscape and not a suitable place to hold a national tournament," he claimed. "First of all it lacks facilities. The clubhouse is inadequate and in fact it would be a farce if

The annual invitation tournament at the Newport Casino. Here Williams is beating McLoughlin, far court.

68

held there." Among Hopkins's supporters was William Clothier, the influential Philadelphian.

No one today would deny that Forest Hills lacks facilities. It lacks space. It lacks lavatories. There is no sensible traffic arrangement in the local streets, which were in fact designed for the purpose of keeping traffic out. The inadequacy of the clubhouse is not much of an argument, because it is only used by a few hundred people and was never intended to be a large gathering place. It may be that the old Merion Cricket Club was sneering at the pale imitation of its own clubhouse, also half-timbered Tudor but much more expansive. At any rate, despite the limitations, Forest Hills has never been a farce.

The response to Hopkins's proclamation was hardly unanimous in Philadelphia itself. Of thirteen clubs that spoke up, eight were for New-

James Van Alen, Newport scion, organizer of the Tennis Hall of Fame, at Eton College, England, in 1966. Note the letters VASSS on the cup, for Van Alen Simplified Scoring System, out of which came the tie breaker.

port, five for New York. The vote at the USLTA meeting would be close. Actually, only ten votes swung the decision for Forest Hills. In the balloting Harry Seymour of Pittsburgh threw a decisive vote to New York and others followed. The vote was 129–119 for the West Side. In a spirit of reconciliation it was officially made unanimous to hold the 1915 nationals at New York. Women's singles and doubles would be played at Merion, and the Pittsburgh Athletic Club lost to Lakewood Club the right to hold the national clay-court tournament. The meeting was characterized by an unusually high attendance and very few proxies.

At this time the USLTA had the task of scheduling no less than 167 official tournaments between March and October. In the New York area alone there were 25,000 tennis players. This concentration suggested to worried officials an enormous number of entries in the championships, as predicted by Newport supporters—as many as 1,000! Newport's largest entry list had been 212. The executive committee met on March 21 and decreed that there would be no limit on the number so long as the entries were submitted by clubs, thereby making the clubs weed out mediocre players. Furthermore, the entry fee would be set high enough to prevent cheapskates from entering just to get a seat at the tournament at a lower price and then defaulting.

As the time to open the West Side courts approached, the club felt justified in leasing property off Central Park West at 92nd and 93rd Streets for courts for members who did not want to go out to Forest Hills. So for a short time the members had the best of both worlds. The only cloud on the horizon was the warning in the spring of 1915 that the USLTA would be accepting bids from other cities wanting the nationals in 1916. The West Side officers therefore impressed on the tournament committee, headed by the indefatigable Julian Myrick, the importance of putting on such an impressive show that no competing club would be able to wrest the nationals from the grasp of Long Island.

6

EFFICIENT
AND SCIENTIFIC
ARRANGEMENTS

WE LIKE TO THINK that the popularity of tennis is a fad of the 1970s, but in 1915 tennis received much more attention in *The New York Times*, for example, than it does today. Readers that summer could follow not only the big matches at Sea Bright, Longwood, Rye and Newport, but those of the University Heights Tennis Club, where a Cornell boy named Francis T. Hunter won the cup (eventually he rose to rank second in the nation after Tilden). Half the sports page on July 8 was taken up with reports on tournaments at the Nassau Country Club, Siwanoy Country Club in Westchester, the finals at Elmhurst in Westchester and the progress of the East–West matches at the California Tennis Club in San Francisco.

This same day Robert D. Wrenn, who had ranked number one in the country for four years during the nineties, speaking as president of the USLTA, told a reporter about "the efficient and scientific basis of arrangements at the West Side Tennis Club" for the national championships at the end of August. This was an obvious dig at Newport. The *Times* said that Mr. Myrick had arranged for "perfect surveying" of the twenty-four courts, as if in the past they had been laid out haphazardly elsewhere.

The pretournament publicity was skillfully scheduled to whet the public appetite. On July 29 it was announced that wooden stands for 7,000 were under construction, requiring 140,000 square feet of lumber. Each spectator would have 18 inches of space to sit on. This information was the final straw for a public that had been informed it would be allowed to buy tickets at the matches only for places not subscribed by members of clubs belonging to the USLTA.

On August 2 Wrenn hastily reversed this decision and opened the sale of tickets to everyone in order "to place the lovers of the game and the memberships of the clubs upon the same basis without any partiality." The tickets, he added, could be had at the office of Harry Parker, the committee member in charge of selling them, in downtown Manhattan. No ticket agencies handled the seats to the nationals then. At the time 2,000 tickets had already been sold, but probably Wrenn had concluded that not enough club members would subscribe and the public would be too annoyed to take its chances on buying tickets at Forest Hills. This was really the only gaffe in the "efficient and scientific arrangements." The price of tickets for the entire tournament was $5. General-admission seats were to be sold at 50 cents per day.

The buildup continued on August 8, when 200 players entered the national preliminaries at Sea Bright, Newport and the Meadow Club at Southampton. "There will be general satisfaction," *The New York Times* commented, "if the fates make it possible for McLoughlin to play Williams in the final round, and with the Westerner thirsting for revenge these two should have a battle royal." The fates did not make it possible, for Mc-Loughlin's game had gone off since his defeat of Brookes a year ago.

The problem of too large an entry list never really developed. Some 200 players wanted to play at Forest Hills, but 128 is the maximum for national championships. Myrick simply stuck to the USLTA "clubs only" rule, and he wound up with a draw of the right size on August 24. Among the players were Frank Hunter and Walter Pate, later captain of the Davis Cup team. Tilden, though already twenty-one, did not enter.

"Forest Hills is really the centre of the tennis world of this country," *The New York Times* remarked. Meanwhile at Newport an invitation tournament was being held in the busiest week of the social season, "with no end of parties and dinner dances," a social reporter noted. The loss of the championship had really done Newport no harm. It was but a momentary blow to community pride.

The first nationals at Forest Hills were scheduled to start on August 30. The day before, *The New York Times* filled its sports page with pictures of T. R. Pell, George Church, Harold A. Throckmorton, H. H. Hackett, Frederick B. Alexander, Karl Behr, Craig Biddle, Richard Norris Williams, Wallace F. Johnson, Charles M. Bull, Jr., and Watson M. Washburn. McLoughlin was for unexplained reasons missing from this gallery of stars. In one year he had declined precipitously, although his publishers, advertising his book, quoted the Boston *Herald's* comment: "McLoughlin is probably the greatest player in the world today."

William M. Johnston was said to be the best of the Western players, and Williams, weak on clay and asphalt, was predicted to win on turf that week.

"The National Championship is a test of the survival of the fittest," a Darwinian sportswriter wrote in *The New York Times.*

Alas, on the thirtieth it rained, and the familiar sight of tarpaulin being dragged across the grass was witnessed by disconsolate players and officials, 150 of whom had attended an inaugural dinner given by the West Side Tennis Club at the Hotel Vanderbilt in town. But the postponement did not dim the success of the opening day on August 31, when sixty-one matches were played before a crowd of about 5,000, who wandered from court to court and came into the stands for the big matches.

There was a legion of West Side officials, identifiable by the dark green hatbands on their straw hats with thin red, white and blue stripes in the middle. In those days men almost invariably wore boaters. Officials wore badges of different colors to distinguish their functions, a practice continued to this day. To impress upon everyone how "efficient and scientific" this tournament could be, Myrick deployed a band of roving umpires to check up on the officiating and to pay particular attention to foot faults.

The crowd was rewarded the first day with one exciting five-set match in which N. W. Niles beat Alexander, whose exertions carried him at one point so far off to the side that he smashed a glass of ginger ale on a table as he swung at the ball. To celebrate the opening, a theater party for 200 players and officials was arranged at the Park Theatre, where *13 Washington Square* with May Irwin was playing. Such a pleasant diversion would be unlikely today, as players and officials are scattered, and Broadway in late August has little allure.

On September 2 a *New York Times* headline read:

GERMANY GIVES A WRITTEN PROMISE TO SINK NO LINERS WITHOUT WARNING

The war had become global. The *Lusitania* had been sunk in May. No players from Europe or the British Empire were in the tournament. But Europe was seven days away by boat in those years and the war was like a fairy tale to most Americans, who were naturally on the side of the Allies. The year 1915 was a desperate one in France, but the United States was having its most successful lawn-tennis season.

The second day of the tournament saw the longest set in the history of the nationals; W. M. Hall beat Wallace Johnson 18–16, and took the match in an upset over the chop-stroke artist of the period. There were no complaints about the time it took. It was a less hurried age, and the tie breaker would not have been welcome to that patient crowd. But there were complaints about the wear and tear on the turf, especially on the center courts, where the grandstands stood. This problem was not to be dealt with definitively until the decision in 1974 to play the Open on Har-tru clay surfaces.

If the players were bothered, the crowds were not, and they came in such numbers that the Long Island Railroad added an extra train to relieve the congestion. Their favorite was McLoughlin, whom they rushed to see wherever he played. He was conspicuous off the court for the enormous, spectacular polo coat he wore in 80-degree weather.

More college players competed then—from Penn, Harvard, Columbia, Princeton and the like. Tennis was still very much an amateur sport, a gentleman's game. Still, the shamateurism of modern times was developing; manufacturers sought endorsements for tennis equipment, and clubs picked up expenses in order to get the best players to enter their tournaments. The hypocrisy was beginning. There was as yet no open playing for money. A tennis pro then, like the West Side's famous George Agutter, was a teacher, not a player recompensed from gate receipts. Golf, which got started in America a few years later than tennis, was always an open sport, from the first national tournament in 1895. This allowed amateurs like Bobby Jones to play pros like Walter Hagen. It took almost a century for the tennis world to adopt this sensible arrangement.

As the 1915 matches proceeded, there were upsets and disquieting evidence that the reigning champion, Williams, was not going to get to the finals. Not content with playing his regular matches, he put on an exhibition with an average player, J. A. Adoue, Jr., whom he managed to beat, albeit unimpressively. The derogatory comments could not have helped his morale—he said he was just taking it easy because of the heat. But it was only 80 degrees, and in the semifinals he succumbed in five sets to the diminutive Californian William M. Johnston, a man he had beaten in straight sets at Longwood. Williams's overconfidence took the coy form of kissing his fingers to the ball when his 120-pound opponent passed him, a practice he abandoned in the fourth set.

Johnston faced McLoughlin in the finals, the first all-Western finals of the championships. The crowd of 9,000 could not have hoped for a more stirring finish to a tournament that, it was agreed, surpassed all previous nationals in the quality of play. McLoughlin found himself facing a faster player with a forehand the likes of which he had never seen before. That someone as small as Johnston could hit so hard was psychologically disconcerting. The Comet's own game lacked fire, and something of the zip was gone from his serve. Johnston was described with a variety of metaphors: he had the "eye of an eagle," he moved "like a cat," and even on occasions "like chained lightning." In desperation McLoughlin ran around his backhand, to which Johnston deliberately played. Shots McLoughlin thought were winners were retrieved by Johnston, and it was then too late to go after the ball.

"It was run, run, run for McLoughlin," said *The New York Times*. Although he won the first set 6–1, he dropped the next three and then dropped from exhaustion, as did Johnston, and the joyous throng carried both players from the court on their shoulders.

Johnston's victory, deserved though it was, was overshadowed by the lingering hero worship of McLoughlin, and he was not yet the adored "Little Bill" so revered by Tilden. He became, in the words of George Lott, "the most popular tennist ever to step on a court." But at this time he was more part of the colorful new background of Forest Hills than the principal actor in a drama. New York had found a new level of tennis rather than a new hero to worship.

The general response to the success of the first championship at Forest Hills was overwhelming. Julian Myrick was not forgotten amid the uproar. "From every side could be heard expressions of satisfaction at the general arrangements, and congratulations of the highest order were showered upon Mr. Julian Myrick and his corps of able assistants for their splendid work," wrote F. B. Alexander in the *Spalding Lawn Tennis Annual.* Alexander was one of the players put out by McLoughlin at Forest Hills.

The New York Times editorialized:

> Tennis as it is played today has found a new place in the field of sports. . . . The game has been played more generally in the West than in the East. In the vicinity of Los Angeles a suburban home is not complete without its tennis court. . . . New York is just beginning to learn how much this means in the way of healthy exercise and to imitate California by planting tennis courts in every conceivable place where a vacant lot large enough for a court can be found. Thus New York may produce more potential tennis champions in the future as the game becomes more generally known here. . . . Not long ago the champions were middle aged men. . . . The crowds not the players however demonstrated the most important thing about tennis at the Forest Hills tournament. . . . More than 7000 persons witnessed these games it was estimated. Only a few years ago the national championships were witnessed by only a handful of spectators.

The 7,000 referred to one day's crowd. Probably 30,000 attended the tournament. However, only a small crowd turned out two days later for the East–West matches in which McLoughlin beat Behr. As the big-name players departed, those lingering at the bar were discussing Charlie Bull's promise that the next year perhaps the nationals would be played at the Crescent Athletic Club in neighboring Brooklyn. And others said that Longwood had developed an appetite for the event. It was apparent that success in staging a tournament meant no more from year to year than success in winning the championship itself. Forest Hills had no guarantee of its future for such matches—yet.

7

WAR YEARS

THE WEST SIDE'S FEAR of losing the nationals was premature. For the next five years the club kept the championship privilege, until the Germantown Cricket Club was able to get enough votes at the USLTA meeting for the men's nationals in 1921, 1922 and 1923. During those years the West Side could still boast the women's nationals and the Davis Cup challenge round, both of which drew huge crowds.

During the war years of 1916 to 1918 there was no Davis Cup or international play, and the Japanese were the only foreign players at Forest Hills tournaments. The United States declared war on Germany in April 1917. By summer many of the best players were in uniform, and that year the nationals were canceled. In their place a National Patriotic Tournament was held at the West Side for the benefit of the Red Cross ambulance service. In 1918, shortly before the Armistice bill, Tilden made his first appearance as a finalist at Forest Hills—and lost in straight sets to R. L. Murray, not one of the most memorable players.

Despite the war, the 1916 men's championship was an even bigger success than the initial one at Forest Hills. It is clear to see why the USLTA again awarded the tournament to the West Side Club. The club was able to give the USLTA $10,000 and still report a $75,000 surplus and assets of more than $150,000. At this time initiation fees were raised from $50 to $75 for new members, and dues from $25 to $35 annually. A successful national was as good as money in the pockets of club members. These figures are rather hard to judge now, but it may be helpful to note that at the time the Forest Hills Inn was running little ads in the papers mentioning seventy-five trains a day and rates from $15 a week!

The summer of 1916 in America was one of blissful ignorance of the consequences of what the headlines were full of: Germany's defeat of Russia and the prefiguring of revolution in Petrograd. Among those listed as buying boxes for the Newport Invitation Tournament that season was the Russian ambassador, together with the Drexels, the Astors, Livingstons, Van Alens, Auchinclosses and dozens of other socially prominent people. And Newport was not the only attraction for society. From the West Side Club, which had made such heavy going of the superficiality of Newport's crowds, names of the best people buying boxes were released to the press. Said *The New York Times:*

> The social world is out in force. . . . The women folks were all resplendent in summer finery and the grand stand showed great patches of color from silken jackets and hats of many hues. . . . One of the debutantes remarked the courts were smooth enough to dance on.

Among the spectators was Theodore Roosevelt, who held forth for reporters on the clubhouse porch and revealed the secret of his tennis cabinet:

> I was president and Ambassador Jusserand was vice president. Anyone who defeated either Jusserand or myself was under the rules forever barred from membership.

The French ambassador was a scholar who included the history of tennis among his subjects.

The 1916 setting was described by *The New York Times:*

COURTS A VAST MOTION PICTURE

> It would be a hard task to find a better place for the tournament than Forest Hills. There it is, set on the Long Island plains just like a little spotless town. The village with its quaint looking houses and red-roofed gables looks for all the world like an old English hamlet.

It was easier to describe the panorama than to draw up a form sheet on the players that summer. Interlocking defeats on the grass circuit defied prediction, and there were no favorites. Although J. Parmely Paret, one of the leading tennis writers, had written in *American Lawn Tennis* that Johnston, who had just turned twenty-one, "possesses skill, agility and endurance unequalled on the courts," Johnston's recent upset at Newport by the Japanese Ichiya Kumagae baffled all seers.

Williams had wrenched his ankle at Newport, so the word was that Murray, a Californian transplanted to Niagara Falls, might wind up in the finals against Kumagae. McLoughlin was no longer considered a contender. Tilden was eliminated by Throckmorton.

Kumagae did not reach the third round. He was beaten in straight sets by Church, who went on to beat McLoughlin in four sets and then lose to Murray in five. Kumagae, an exotic figure and the only foreigner playing, had been besieged by photographers for a day. McLoughlin still drew crowds even playing mediocre tennis, but once he was out of it, Johnston became the attraction, and for the semifinals 12,000 people came, the biggest crowd since the Brookes–McLoughlin Davis Cup match. Johnston easily beat Murray and came into the finals against Williams favored to hold his title. Williams had beaten Griffin, Johnston's doubles partner, who held with him the national doubles championship that had been played off in a one-match challenge round at the beginning of the singles tournament.

The five-set final was as good as any match yet played in the history of the championships. Williams, despite having a weak ankle and being down two sets to one, took the fourth set. Methodical and not flashy, he fell behind quickly 3–0 in the fifth set, and it looked like the little champion would win another love set and the match. But in fact he had shot his bolt. The endurance Paret claimed for him was at an end. Yet at 5–4 Johnston staved off two match points with such desperation that his force vanished, and on the next to last point he lost his grip and his racket flew out of his hand as he poked at the ball. He dumped a backhand in the net and Williams again had his name inscribed on the trophy he had won two years before. And Johnston had lost the first of six national finals he appeared in at Forest Hills. Of eight finals this remarkable player reached (two were played at Germantown) he was able to win only in 1915 and in 1919, the latter being the only time he beat Tilden for the championship.

Williams, raised and trained in Switzerland, had gone to Harvard and represented the East. His win restored the prestige that had slipped away to California after McLoughlin became the champion in 1912 and Johnston in 1915. New York was heady with delight over this conclusion, particularly because of the quality of Johnston's sportsmanship. He showed no bitterness in defeat. Sectionalism was already rife. The West resented the Eastern preponderance in the USLTA and resented a ban on players working in sports stores. McLoughlin and Bundy had started a sports store in San Francisco and the feeling was that they were victims of an injustice. The Pacific Coast chapter had at one point threatened to withdraw from membership in the USLTA, and it named Eastern players who worked for Spalding, Wright & Ditson and department-store sports counters.

The controversy was submerged in the spring of 1917 by the larger event of war. McLoughlin joined the Navy, Johnston went into the Cali-

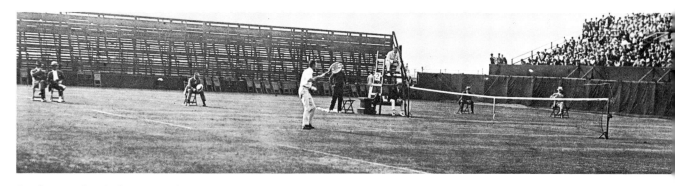

In this eye-level shot from the clubhouse, R. Norris Williams has just volleyed to defending champion Little Bill Johnston's backhand during the 1911 men's national singles at Forest Hills.

fornia militia, and Williams went to Plattsburg for infantry training. Announcing it would raise $100,000 for the Red Cross, the USLTA sanctioned 220 tournaments that season. With so many top players unavailable, Forest Hills under Myrick's magic hand still was able to put on a decent tournament, the National Patriotic Tournament, and eventually to contribute $7,000 to the Red Cross. The draw was cut to sixty-four players. Williams got leave from Plattsburg, but he went down to defeat in the semifinals to a player unranked in 1916, N. W. Niles. The next day Niles lost to Murray in a match played partly in the rain. In the third round Murray beat Bill Tilden in straight sets. Tilden was already twenty-four, and his distinction up to this time was that he had won the national mixed doubles in 1913 and 1914 with Mary K. Browne.

R. Lindley Murray, a lefty, had a serve that carried him past Bill Tilden in straight sets in the 1918 finals.

It rained in the early days, too, and tarpaulins had to be spread over the grass courts by hand.

Another future great appeared during the Patriotic, Molla Bjurstedt, later Mrs. Molla Mallory, who won a series of matches against Mary K. Browne for a trophy offered by Julian Myrick. This foreshadowed the eventual shift of the women's championships from the Philadelphia Cricket Club to New York. Browne was champion in 1913 and 1914, and then Molla dominated the game until Helen Wills came along in 1923.

While the summer's events had proved a success within their limitations, all tournaments combined returned to the ambulance corps of the Red Cross $50,000, half of the goal. While there was satisfaction in having the names of tennis clubs stamped on certain ambulances in France, Julian Myrick as acting president of the USLTA now was concerned for the continuation of the West Side and other clubs because of the war. Ninety-seven members were in the service before the end of 1917, and Myrick sent out a letter to all member clubs of the USLTA urging them to keep the club spirit alive.

If this seems superficial when men were dying in the trenches, it must be remembered that someone who really dedicates himself to an interest is able to exclude all other considerations from his mind. Myrick had no intention of letting the war weaken American tennis, and by keeping a mere sport in the center of his consciousness, he prevented many clubs from getting into financial hot water. They represented "a large property interest," his letter said, and "this must be conserved and built up."

Top: In this view of the field courts, the striped marquee awning is more prominent in the open end of the Stadium bowl.

Bottom: Only press photographers are allowed on the Stadium court. The man in the lower part of the picture is Russ Adams, the official USLTA photographer.

Top opposite: Le ballet du service.

Bottom opposite: Björn Borg.

*Rain is never scheduled,
but in a twelve-day tournament
it is almost
an inevitable feature
of Forest Hills.*

Top right: Informal sportswear has replaced the business suits and boaters of earlier days. In the background is one of the famous concrete eagles.

Top opposite: Field courts, including clubhouse courts, during the 1974 Open. The Stadium is almost empty but the Grandstand to the right is packed.

Bottom opposite: During a first-round match of the 1974 Open, Stan Smith wears a handkerchief on his neck to absorb the perspiration.

Top left and below: Peeking under the green backdrop at the fences is an old Forest Hills custom—among the young.

Right:
The scoreboard outside
the Stadium is an old-
fashioned set
of numerals on cards
changed by hand
from a scaffold.
Under the striped awning
is the air-conditioned
press box.

Above: The ump braces himself
as he fixes his attention
on the service line,
where the ball may be coming in
at 100 m.p.h. or more.

Left: Thousands stand around
field-court matches
in the early rounds of the Open.
In the foreground is the clubhouse terrace.

Opposite: Arthur Ashe,
during the fifth set
of his 1974 match with Newcombe.

Right: The umpire stands out in this view of field court number 8.

Below: A linesman stands to get a better view.

There are other things to pay attention to at Forest Hills besides tennis.

He proposed recruitment of junior members to fill the ranks of those who had gone into war service, and encouraged both boys and girls to play on an equal footing in a game dominated by men. Billie Jean King owes something to Julian Myrick, although if she had known him she probably would have found him as difficult and overbearing as Tilden did. He ran a successful life insurance agency with Charles Ives, the great composer, and he boiled with energy and ambition. At eighty-five he still worked out with dumbbells daily and rallied with a tennis pro despite weakened eyesight.

Before 1917 ended, Myrick had got the War Department to approve the return of national tennis championship tournaments to keep up the physical condition of Americans and to keep "the moral as well as the mental standard up to a high plane," explained the Secretary, Newton D. Baker. Proceeds in 1918 would go to the Commission on Training Camp Activities. The most patriotic tournament, it seemed, was the traditional one. Somewhat disingenuously, the West Side Tennis Club voted to bid for the championships but not to pressure for them if any other club was interested! There was no other club with the will to put on the nationals in wartime. *The New York Times,* on January 20, 1918, interpreted this gesture generously:

> The action of the West Side Club is taken to mean that the organization is ready to stand by the terms of the agreement by which the championships were taken from Newport, namely that the event rotate.

Actually, the idea of rotation was no article of faith at Forest Hills. Myrick explained to club members that it would cause dissension in the USLTA to press for the matches that year. So why press when it was a foregone conclusion that there would be no competition?

At the annual meeting there was some competition behind the scenes over the nomination of Myrick for vice-president of the USLTA. His old opponent from Philadelphia, Hopkins, who was determined to get the matches to his city, was supposed to oppose Myrick, but at the last minute was persuaded not to. Hopkins, of course, did succeed in his determination three years later, and this inspired Myrick to his greatest accomplishment, the building of the Stadium at Forest Hills.

The modesty of the 1918 nationals may be judged by the small grandstand that was put up on one side of the center courts, seating only 1,700. On the opening day, August 26, the Allies were nearing the Hindenberg Line, and Clemenceau was accurately predicting the complete collapse of the enemy. The interest in tennis was minimal. There were no lists of prominent boxholders.

Probably the most interesting (or really the most dull) thing that year was a match lasting eighty-two games. Harold Throckmorton beat Harold Taylor in the second round 6–8, 6–2, 11–9, 7–9, 13–11. Throckmorton, a sergeant on leave, said at the end of the fourth set, "Life in the Army is a perfect cinch compared to this." Next day another match between Seiichio Kashio and G. A. L. Dionne went on for four hours and twenty minutes and was postponed by darkness.

SUN SETS OUT OF SHEER ENNUI, claimed *The New York Times*.

Records showed that not since 1888, when Presbrey and Tailer toiled eighty-two games for five hours, had such lengthy matches been played. A spectator watching Kashio suggested the match would only be stopped when they had to mow the grass. As if chained to their respective baselines, the players kept the ball going across the net as many as 122 times. For the record, Kashio won when play resumed next day.

The favorites were Murray and Tilden. Tilden was the clay-court champion that year and was improving, though still unranked. In the semifinals he knocked off fifth-ranking Kumagae in straight sets, and it seemed that he should beat the champion, Murray, who had not competed that season and was playing only to help give the tournament a bit of class and to swell the gate receipts for a worthy cause. But Tilden had a boil on his ankle and Murray was at the top of his form, playing the California big-game style, putting Tilden on the defensive and moving him around the court with ease. It was over in three sets and Murray retained his title 6–3, 6–1, 7–5. In a world in which it was reported that a girl had assassinated Lenin, no one could get very excited over this tepid tennis. It did raise $8,000 for the War Department.

So the first five years of big-time tennis at Forest Hills ended with something of a whimper. Six weeks after the nationals, Congress passed the War-time Prohibition Act, a harbinger of the Roaring Twenties. At the West Side, that era really began in 1919.

Many tennis stars joined the military during World War I. This group happens to be all Army. From left to right: Lt. Col. Dwight Davis of Davis Cup fame; Maj. R. D. Wrenn, national champion of the nineties; Maj. W. A. Larned, a ranking player; Capt. Watson Washburn, another ranking player; Capt. Norris Williams, the first champion of Forest Hills; Capt. D. S. Watters, who got to the quarterfinals at Forest Hills in 1916; Lt. Dean Mathey, member of the West Side, ranked ten in 1916; and Col. W. F. Johnson, chop-stroke artist of the early twenties.

PART II

MATURING : 1919-1941

8

FIRST BATTLE
OF THE BILLS

ANTICIPATING A RENEWED POSTWAR ENTHUSIASM for tennis, the West Side Club started the year 1919 with the announcement of plans to add two wings to the clubhouse. Its members learned at the annual meeting that 167 of their number had done military duty and five had been killed at the front. In awarding the nationals again to Forest Hills, the USLTA looked forward to the most active tennis season in history. Not only would demobilization return players to competition, but the international character of the game, heightened in interest by the strong relationships arising out of the European war, would be restored. At Cannes in March the YMCA put on a tournament in which three American titlists played: Williams, Larned and Wrenn. The Wimbledon champion from Australia, Gerald Patterson, planned to play at Forest Hills, as did other Australians and Japanese.

A sign of how well organized tennis had become was the growth to 600 of the National Umpires Association membership, and the West Side asked that 150 of these be appointed for the opening matches. Until this time the club's members had been the bulk of the umpire staff. Given this new power, the chairman of the umpires' association pontificated to what he must have presumed to be a public utterly ignorant of spectator behavior. In a statement to the press Edward C. Conlin told the crowd such fundamental things as to remain seated during play, to keep quiet, not to applaud during a rally and never to applaud errors. Don't coach the players or scold officials, he admonished.

"The players don't kick, for they know that any errors of judgment generally even themselves in the course of a match," he said. Obviously he had never umpired a match with Tilden playing. He reminded all that tennis was an amateur sport played for fun.

Symbolic of this pompousness was a new umpire's chair for the center court that drew all kinds of derision and was called variously "the tank," "the armored car," "the water tower" and "the lighthouse." It was described as having a basement and an attic, and its side boxes were verandas. Equipment mysteriously included tongue scrapers, garters, safety pins, a buttonhook, a shoehorn and a supply of lemons. To make himself better heard in a time when there was no public address system, the umpire had a megaphone. (Incidentally, all officials are umpires, whether linesmen, net-cord judges or umpires in the chair. The referee is in charge of the umpires and the matches and does not officiate directly. One of his chief responsibilities is to decide when play should be stopped because of weather or darkness. On August 25, 1919, for instance, the tournament opening was postponed a day because of rain. On the twenty-seventh, despite showers, play continued. It was Wimbledon weather.)

In the rain Williams, wearing his Harvard varsity sweater, beat young Vinnie Richards, who competed in both the juniors and men's singles. Richards had very nearly beaten Tilden in the winter at the Middle Atlantic Covered-Court Tournament in Philadelphia in a match considered the greatest played in that city. Leading 5–1 in the fifth set, the younger player, a protégé of Tilden's, ran out of energy, and the man who was being increasingly talked about as a great player won the set 7–5.

McLoughlin, past his prime, was still the most popular player at Forest Hills, but he succumbed early and it came down to whether Patterson, the Wimbledon champ, could beat Johnston in the semis. Some say this five-set struggle won by Johnston was a greater match than the Brookes–McLoughlin Davis Cup classic. Patterson lost the final point on a bad bounce, but Johnston had obviously beaten him and would face Tilden, the victor in five sets over Kumagae.

"The two Williams of tennis royalty will meet tomorrow for the title of William the Conqueror," said *The New York Times.*

Two columns were devoted to a review of the games of this Mutt-and-Jeff pair who were to be national finalists no less than six times in what came to be known as the Battle of the Bills—Little Bill Johnston and Big Bill Tilden. Johnston at five-feet-seven was actually only an inch shorter than Rod Laver, but he was of small build. Tilden stood six-two.

Two days of rain caused successive postponements, and to prevent the grass from being smothered beneath the tarpaulin, hay was laid down under it to let air circulate. Reporters hung around George Agutter, the

Tilden looked elegant on court, but he was generally sloppy in dress and untidy by habit.

club professional, who liked to pose holding fourteen balls in his left hand and forearm. George told them how to hit a backhand, what causes tennis elbow, why touch is so important in tennis, and said that Vinnie Richards's swing finished too high. He warned average players against modeling their game on those of some champions like Patterson, who could get away with an unorthodox backhand that the hacker would never master.

Among the umpires for the match were the third-ranking Alexander, eighth-ranking Garland, a veteran finalist, Wright, and the tennis reporter S. H. "Pop" Merrihew, publisher of *American Lawn Tennis* magazine. Woodrow Wilson was starting his unsuccessful national tour to sell the League of Nations to the country. Tilden, having beaten Johnston three times in the season, was expected to win the title and was already being called the greatest player of all time.

The judgment was premature. He went down in straight sets as Johnston again won the title he held in 1915. Johnston had finally spotted Tilden's weakness, a backhand that was totally defensive, hit invariably with underspin. As Johnston pounded away at that weakness, Tilden tried every shot he had in order to get at his little jackrabbit opponent. But having such a huge repertoire of shots, the famous all-round game, was a handicap because it led to indecision. Tilden was by far the more spectacular of the two, and he was famous for getting the impossible gets. Yet he lost to a more aggressive and craftier player who dominated the net and gave Tilden few opportunities to win from the baseline. Johnston's backhand was not as strong as his blinding forehand, but it was an aggressive stroke that gave no comfort to Tilden. In desperation Tilden took to lobbing, but his lobs lacked depth, and Johnston turned them into winners. The final shot was a gentle tap beyond Tilden's reach.

87

Tilden fans were disappointed and so was Tilden. Here he was twenty-six, a year older than Johnston, who first won the title at twenty. Perhaps the two days of rain and a soggy surface had taken the edge off his game. Yet the next day at Forest Hills in matches with Australia (with nothing at stake; America did not enter Davis Cup competition in 1919) Tilden beat the great Patterson and teamed with Johnston to win the doubles despite their total inability to work as a team. Both would be covering the same side of the court, leaving the other half wide open. Somehow they would scramble back to position. Not for nothing was Tilden sometimes described as the world's worst doubles partner.

Tilden, like many great athletes, was high-strung, nervous, temperamental and physically fragile. He was something of a spoiled brat, given to outbursts of anger on the court—not a clown like Nastase, but annoying enough at times to earn the crowd's displeasure. Fantastic to watch, he was not always lovable. But he had whatever it is that makes a champion. Call it will, for one thing. Seeing in the cold light of reflection how Johnston had made him look feeble on the backhand, he determined to remake that stroke completely. Rarely, if ever, are such efforts successful. Season after season Frank Parker, with one of the great backhands, introduced a new forehand without developing a stroke he or anyone else admired.

William Tatem Tilden II had the leisure and money to do what he pleased. His father was a Philadelphia wool merchant and a civic figure, chairman of the executive committee of the Business Man's League of Penn-

Warren Harding dutifully receives the Davis Cup team of 1921 at the White House. The players, left to right, were: Watson Washburn, Samuel Hardy (non-playing captain), Wallace Johnson and Tilden. Second from the left is the famous Forest Hills enthusiast Julian Myrick.

The cast of the most famous duel in Forest Hills history: William T. Tilden II and William Johnston, before their last match in 1925. Little Bill cagily posed a step higher, hoping to conceal his shortness from the photographer.

In the twenties Bill Tilden was Forest Hills. He reigned like a king among the monarchs of the Golden Age of Sport—Babe Ruth, Bobby Jones, Gene Tunney.

sylvania and a member of the Board of Public Education. His mother was a pianist. Bill, a second son, was born in 1893 and was privately tutored until he was fifteen. He had learned tennis from his brother, and at eight he won a tournament for boys under fifteen. But he was slow to develop into a national competitor. Because the women's championships and mixed doubles were played in Philadelphia, Mary K. Browne, the titleholder, got young Tilden to be her partner in 1913 and they won the title. But mixed doubles is not serious. Turned down for military service for flat feet, Tilden continued to plug away at a game that combined serves and overheads of blinding speed with spinning ground strokes.

He got to the finals twice at Forest Hills, and all the time he studied the game more intensely than any living player. Tennis was his passion. It is true that he tried his hand at acting and was in a few bad Broadway plays, but he did not put his heart and soul into the theater.

In his classic book *Match Play and the Spin of the Ball* (reissued in 1969), Tilden displays a complete understanding of the games of all the good players from the beginning of the century, calls Brookes the first all-court player, which for Tilden is the model, and Williams "the connecting link between the passing style and the one to come." The one to come was of course Tilden's own game, which dominated world tennis for more than a decade.

Whether he was the greatest player of all time, as is often claimed by some players and observers, is not possible to establish. Unlike great performances of musical works, which can be recorded and compared to each other with some objectivity, the only fair judgment of a tennis player's comparative merit is to match him with someone great. Tilden was too old to play competitively against Budge, Perry, Kramer and Gonzales. He died before Rod Laver was an international player. But in his time Tilden, though not invincible, was Mister Tennis. And what finally put him there was a new backhand which he fashioned painfully in Providence, Rhode Island. After the end of the 1919 season he let himself be persuaded to coach the son of J. D. E. Jones, an insurance executive for the Equitable Life Insurance Company who happened to have his own indoor tennis court.

To avoid the charge of professionalism, Tilden took no money for the lessons but was on the payroll of the company. No doubt his name was helpful in getting the firm business. But Tilden, with his independent means, was in Providence because of that indoor court.

All fall and winter he worked out on a backboard and played with local players to get rid of the slice backhand and substitute a flat shot. To strengthen his arms he chopped wood. He allowed himself to be humiliated in exhibitions with men not in his class. The New England champion, Harte, beat him in East Providence in four sets. But after several months of this punishment he emerged from hibernation in New England with a new weapon that completed his variety of shots. In April he took the national indoor title from Richards in straight sets at the Seventh Regiment Armory. During this match he blew up when a foot fault was declared against him and deliberately hit the next two serves out in childish fury.

He could also be generous in throwing points when a bad call was made against an opponent. This form of sportsmanship was imitated by Budge until von Cramm pointed out that it humiliated the umpire and was not necessarily appreciated by the opponent.

In the summer Tilden went to England and beat all opponents at Wimbledon, winning the right to challenge the champion, Patterson, while Johnston fared poorly. Although his right knee had been weakened by a pulled ligament, Tilden beat Patterson in five sets, and the interesting thing is that he won by pounding Patterson's backhand. The Australian took the backhand with the same face of the racket he used on the forehand! (Try this and see what a strain it is on the wrist.)

Gradually Tilden's persistence turned Patterson's wrist limp. His performance earned him the title of world champion, an honor granted to Wimbledon by the International Lawn Tennis Federation. The sportswriters called him the best player in the world, and after winning his Davis Cup matches against France and England he returned to New York, hailed as one of the greatest players of all time.

In losing the first Battle of the Bills in 1919, he had been forced to find himself, to admit his inadequacy and to overcome it. He was now ready for whatever awaited him at Forest Hills, and it turned out again to be a man for whom he had the deepest admiration and affection, Little Bill Johnston.

9

ENGINE FAILURE

THE 1920 FINALS between Tilden and Johnston provided some of the greatest moments in the history of Forest Hills tennis. But the day was marred by a ghastly fatality. One of the technical advances of the war was the mass production of airplanes and the sudden appearance in the skies of droning, slow-moving biplanes with open cockpits. They were a novelty, and barnstorming pilots could make a living stunting for crowds that paid to see aerial gymnastics—and morbidly awaited a crash.

On August 25, 1919, at Sea Girt, New Jersey, a Navy lieutenant crashed while stunting at 300 feet for a crowd of 1,000. On July 11, 1920, a similar accident occurred at Salisbury Beach in Massachusetts.

While Johnston and Tilden were playing their match on September 6, 1920, before a crowd of 10,000, a Navy two-seater appeared over the courts at the beginning of the third set and, to the annoyance of the crowd, began making low passes. It came in at 500 feet, and a man leaned out of the rear cockpit with a camera. The plane pulled up to 900 feet and dropped this time to 300. The spectators were furious.

It rose to 500 feet. The plane's motor suddenly sputtered and stopped. The plane hung almost motionless for a moment, started to glide and plunged to earth a few hundred feet from the stands in a vacant lot. Tilden had been about to serve. The famous umpire E. C. Conlin was in the chair.

Fearing a panic, he turned to Johnston and said, "Can you go on?" Johnston nodded. Conlin looked at Tilden, who also nodded and took his place at the baseline. "Play!" roared the umpire.

According to Tilden's recollection, only 50 people left the stands to see the wreck. But how would he know? He was playing tennis. The papers reported that 3,000 left, which seems an exaggeration, for such a mass exit would surely have disturbed the players. What those who reached the wreck saw was a Navy plane that had been sent from Mitchell Field to take pictures of the match for recruiting purposes.

In other words, the pilot, Lieutenant James Murray Grier, who happened to come from a prominent family in Tilden's Philadelphia, was taking chances for his photographer, Sergeant Joseph Saxe. Presumably Saxe, who had admittedly broken all regulations to get pictures of the *Resolute* and the *Shamrock IV* at the America's Cup races off Newport, was taking exciting shots in order to entice young men into a peacetime Army career that included training as an aerial photographer.

Saxe was one of the leaders in his profession, but he was foolhardy. At Mitchell Field mechanics had warned the pair that the plane's motor was old and not up to much stunting. As a result of this accident the regulations about flying over cities were considerably tightened.

Prior to the matches that year the stuffier side of tennis manifested itself in an official pronouncement. The directors of the tournament, evidently fed up with the casualness of the players, warned them that they would be defaulted if they reported to the referee's desk more than ten minutes late. When Dean Mathey was so tied up on business that he could not get through to the clubhouse by telephone, he was defaulted. Told to hurry up, Fred Alexander, who had ranked number three in 1918 and who was both an umpire and an active promoter of tennis at the West Side, told them to go to hell and let himself be defaulted.

A more serious pronouncement came from Julian Myrick, now finally president of the USLTA. He stiffly reminded everyone that the matches would determine the *national* champion, not the *world* champion:

> Since Mr. Tilden's notable victory at Wimbledon he has been acclaimed the "world's champion" by reason of the fact that such title was awarded perpetually to England by the International Lawn Tennis Federation.
>
> Seeing that the United States is not a member of the federation because it opposes this perpetual award of a championship of any country, it cannot in justice claim that one of its players holds the world's championship. No matter whether an American won or lost at Wimbledon, the position of the USLTA must be the same in fairness to all concerned and it would be particularly unsportsmanlike for us to claim the title when an American won the tournament in question.

93

Some perennials who flourished at Forest Hills in the twenties and thirties:

Frank Hunter.

Frank Shields.

This attitude of course does not detract from the credit due to Mr. Tilden for his fine victory won against the best players of the leading tennis nations. Since the Davis Cup team won the right to challenge Australia for the cup and since they will all be playing at Forest Hills, it may also be said with entire truth that the winner of this tournament will doubtless be considered the best player in the world this year. The world's singles championship is not at stake however so far as the USLTA is concerned in its management of this tournament.

The press ignored this, and when Tilden won, the papers crowned him king of the courts. Yet Myrick won the argument. Two years later Wimbledon dropped its claim and the United States joined the ILTF, which had been formed in 1913. (The president of the ILTF in 1974 is an American, Walter Elcock of Brookline, Massachusetts.)

The history of tennis would probably take too long to recount if it included many of the matches played before the finals. But some of the best tennis at Forest Hills is played in the earlier rounds, and the finals are sometimes a letdown. In 1920 two great quarterfinals were played in succession as Tilden beat Richards and Johnston beat Williams. Tilden's was a particularly crushing victory.

Sidney Wood.   *George Lott.*

Vinnie Richards, a student at Fordham, looked on Tilden as his coach, and he was frequently able to make Tilden play badly. He boasted before this match that the 4 to 1 odds in Tilden's favor were ridiculous and that he would win. In fact Tilden for once just toyed with his pupil and doubles partner, beating him 6–0 in the final set. Johnston and Williams replayed their thrilling 1916 finals, but Williams twisted his ankle in the third set and lost speed. Johnston was so unconcerned on the last point that he did not realize he had won the match and was preparing to serve again.

Tilden reached the finals without any real test. Johnston had to fight almost all the way. This happened because there was still no seeding in tournaments and the luck of the draw determined everything. So far no top players had ever been forced to meet in the earliest rounds. The fairness of the system was emphasized by Myrick, who pointed out that a dozen people were involved in making the drawing in front of a crowd of newspapermen.

If Johnston was tired, Tilden was nursing a sore knee, having wrenched it at Southampton ten days earlier. September 6 was a cloudy day and rain threatened. The crowd was described as exhibiting a mob spirit and was not above razzing the officials. There were bad calls. There was the plane crash. But the tennis was outstanding and Tilden required five sets to prove

95

his superiority under these strange conditions. He got to match point at 5–4, serving in the fourth set, when a cloudburst caused the stands to erupt with screams and move for shelter. In the confusion Tilden, after putting the ball in play, simply did not go after the return, assuming a let. The umpire confirmed the assumption. Let ball. The players left the court at once. On returning, however, they were informed that the referee, George Adee, had overruled the umpire, Conlin, and Johnston was awarded the point. Tilden argued for five minutes and Conlin said he would support a protest at the annual meeting of the USLTA if Tilden lost the match.

As if the protest were more important than winning, Tilden then served three double faults in a row. When they were at match point again, Johnston retrieved a smash that Tilden considered so improbable that he was startled out of going after it. Tilden took the final set 6–3. In the stroke analysis it was his serve that stood out: he had twenty aces, Johnston had none. But Johnston was master at the net, and modern analysts believe that Tilden's modest volleying capacity would make it possible for many of today's players to beat him.

However, Tilden beat the players he had to beat, and at twenty-seven he became one of the legendary figures of the twenties, along with Dempsey, Jones, Ruth, Grange, Sande and Ederle. He won seven national titles, but three of them were not at Forest Hills. The Germantown Cricket Club finally succeeded in getting the nationals away from Forest Hills in 1921, 1922 and 1923. It was a fitting shift from Tilden's point of view, since Germantown was where he learned to play tennis.

To put an end to competing claims from other tennis clubs wanting to hold the national championships, the West Side Tennis Club boldly built the only tennis stadium in the country in the spring of 1924.

George Lott and Lester Stoefen were national doubles champions in 1933 and 1934, but neither ever won the singles title.

10

ENTER THE LADIES

THE STRUGGLE TO GET the men's nationals out of New York came to a climax in the winter of 1921. Early reports had it that the USLTA now favored rotation of this number-one event, but it was doubted that a change would occur immediately. There had been the same doubts when Newport lost the championships. Newport still had the courts, and Boston had adequate facilities for such a tournament, but only Philadelphia pressed the issue, and the USLTA decided to give that city the men's singles and put the ladies'—it was not yet *women's*—singles on at Forest Hills.

Ever since the first ladies' championships in 1887, they had been held at the Philadelphia Cricket Club. The early game was a pretty tame affair played in long hobble skirts and cumbersome hats. The serve was underhand. This may explain how, from 1891 to 1901, the tournament could have ladies playing the best three out of five sets. Characteristic of the lack of vigor in the ladies' game were the six defaults of the finals during the first twenty years.

There has never been a finals default in the history of the men's nationals, and after 1907 only one woman defaulted—Helen Wills Moody, in 1933. But as we shall see, defaulted matches have provided some of the most dramatic events in the annals of women's tennis.

Three players stand out among American women during the second decade of the twentieth century: Hazel Hotchkiss, Mary K. Browne and Molla Bjurstedt. It has been noted how the latter two played an exhibition series at Forest Hills during the war. Hazel Hotchkiss was not in the picture at the time because she had married George Wightman and was raising a family. But she kept playing and was good enough to win the women's doubles with Helen Wills as late as 1928.

The situation in 1921, however, caused attention to focus on the French sensation, young Suzanne Lenglen, who since the war had been rightly acclaimed overseas as the greatest player of her sex. Perhaps in view of the record this did not say much, especially while the war was going on. Women still were overdressed and undermotivated on the courts. But Suzanne was something else. She underdressed and overplayed—in the view of purists. Her dress was not only sleeveless, in place of the customary cuffed blouse, but it was short—just below the knee, pleated to allow the skirt to flow—and had a plunging neckline.

In this costume of liberation the young lady, under the all too watchful prodding of both her parents, literally cavorted on the courts of the Riviera, where she grew up, taking off like a ballet dancer for any shot above her head. She loved to leap and she was a terrible show-off, knowing full well that leaping in that dress was a daring thing to do in those days. But her unorthodox style was effective, and she showed so much power and accuracy that she was unbeatable. In fact it was very difficult for anyone to take a single game from that girl in her prime. She had been trained to hit coins on the court, and she had been trained to win.

Suzanne had no plans to play in America. Wimbledon, which she first won in 1919 at twenty, was as far as she would travel. But an appeal was made to her sense of patriotism by Anne Morgan, a relative of J. P. Morgan, who proposed an exhibition tour of the United States to raise money for the relief of war-damaged western France. Her father was opposed. An attack of bronchitis had weakened her and he feared the effect of a different environment on his sensitive child. He was absolutely right. The trip proved so disastrous that it agitated Suzanne and others for years.

Everything went wrong. First her father got sick. The trip was postponed, but he still refused to go, and he let her go without his blessing. Public expectations were aroused by an eager press. Grantland Rice described her in *Vanity Fair:*

> An amazingly symmetrical figure, replete with grace and litheness, arrayed in a white silk dress that barely flutters below the knees. White silk stockings with white shoes. Above this background of white, hair as black as a raven's wing, bound with a brilliant orange band. Perfectly molded arms, bare and brown from many suns—the entire aspect being one of extreme vividness —an effect immediately to catch and hold the eye.

He had seen her win forty-two games at St. Cloud and lose one—one game, not one set—and he reported that between matches she would change to a crimson headband.

Forest Hills could not resist. A committee beckoned her to play in the nationals there, something she had not intended. Assured that it would be no strain and would pit her against Molla Mallory, the American champion, in the finals, she yielded. Then came the next bit of bad luck. In the unseeded draw she wound up slated to face Mallory in the second round, and when her first-round opponent defaulted, thus depriving her of a warm-up match, it was said by the French that this was a plot to help Mallory win. It was the only time in the history of Forest Hills when the luck of the draw caused what should have been the finals to be played in an early round.

Four days after arriving in New York, four days full of press interviews and giddy adulation, Suzanne came to the West Side in a subdued mood. Her mother wondered whether she should go through with it.

"It would be a calamity to have to quit during the match," she told Suzanne. This may not have been the right thing to say. Children maintain the habit of doing the very opposite of what a parent may suggest long after they are adult. Suzanne was not herself. Instead of resting, though, she spent the afternoon before her match in a box watching the tournament in the hot sun.

Perhaps she liked the thought that the record crowd of 8,000, the largest ever to see ladies' tennis, was paying a lot of attention to her. She was a rather homely girl, people were to observe. But her opponent was not exactly good-looking either. Molla Mallory looked like what she trained to be in her native Norway, a professional masseuse. Swarthy, dark and menacing, she wore a brown sweater over a long white dress.

When play began it was apparent that Mallory was up for the game and Suzanne was not. The American champion had never hit the ball harder and she swept the fragile Suzanne off the court in the first set 6–2. During this startling performance the French girl seemed weak. She made many errors and from time to time coughed. This was the first set she had lost in two years. During the changeover she had a bad coughing fit, but the first point was a long rally that brought some fine shots from her racket before she lost it. She now looked like she might be ready to move into her strong game.

But evidently she was discouraged to find that Molla could take her best shots and still win. She double-faulted. Looking at the umpire, she began to weep. Then she walked to his chair and, speaking French, said she was too ill to go on. The match was defaulted to Mallory, who left for the clubhouse with a round of applause that was only half-hearted. The crowd was unhappy, and after Lenglen disappeared there was audible hissing.

People were disappointed and disillusioned with the Maid Marvel, as some called her. What had happened to Lenglen the Magnificent? It was natural to suppose that she did not want to be beaten for the first time in her career.

MLLE. LENGLEN ILL
WEEPS AND RESIGNS

This was the headline on page 1 of *The New York Times* on August 17. The report said she told the umpire that she was unable to breathe and that she had coughed the night before. People in the club recalled her saying she did not feel like playing, and Sam Hardy, U.S. Davis Cup captain, said that when he had played a practice session with her she seemed lifeless. But despite the clear signs of physical distress, it was not acceptable to default, and for some time in New York the phrase "to cough and quit" was current.

Nor did Suzanne's subsequent behavior help her American reputation. She appeared at Forest Hills the next day and, seemingly in good spirits, chatted with Molla. She continued to attend parties, which gave rise to the charge that she had danced late that night after defaulting. She quit on Molla again in an exhibition at the Crescent Athletic Club.

In New York Suzanne was both naïve and arrogant. And this made good copy. A series of by-lined articles in *The New York Times* carried her personal signature at the bottom. They were lively, well informed and amusing pieces. She listed the questions she had been asked by reporters seeking her opinions on Prohibition (764), short skirts (405), Irish freedom (2), Babe Ruth (72). Who is this *Enfant?* she wondered. To call Babe Ruth "*L'Enfant* Ruth" was endearing.

But she had come to play tennis and she never fulfilled her obligation. In the end she let her adoring public down and slipped back to France having played one mixed doubles exhibition at Forest Hills on September 6 before a crowd of 14,000. Her default followed her home and caused dissension in the French Tennis Federation.

Julian Myrick became involved in a libel threat from Suzanne's lawyers over a letter in which he presumably accused her of being a quitter. Her idea was that Myrick was "pro-*boche*." The whole episode was charged with the emotions generated by the alliance and the terrible war-to-end-all-wars. As long as a year later the controversy flared up again when Lenglen trounced Mallory at Wimbledon 6–2, 6–0. A prominent French sportsman, using the pen name Daninos, wrote critically of the United States' treatment of Lenglen, and the federation chided him. The president of the federation, Henri Wallet, was in his turn denounced for allowing himself to be intimidated by the U.S.A.

Could Lenglen have finished the match with Mallory? Who knows? When she returned to France, her doctors ordered her to take a two-month rest. American doctors who examined her found that she was suffering from the aftereffects of bronchitis. In 1924 she withdrew from Wimbledon after the first round, following recovery from jaundice, and in 1926 she got into a row there and was momentarily defaulted while Queen Mary waited for her to appear.

When she did show up she was trounced by Mrs. J. G. Dewhurst of Ceylon, and that was the end of her amateur career. Clearly she hated

Mary K. Browne practicing in front of the West Side clubhouse.

losing. And what Suzanne wanted, Suzanne got. In her only match with Helen Wills, played at the Carlton Club in Cannes in 1926, the American champion lost in straight sets. Later Wills said, "She won because she was the better player."

She was also unreliable and unpredictable. After a report that she was having a nervous breakdown, she played a match the next day. When she turned pro under the famous Cash-and-Carry Pyle and toured in the United States playing Mary K. Browne in 1927, she got sick and canceled a match in Newark. When she ran into Molla Mallory during the trip, she gave her the cold shoulder. So all in all perhaps Forest Hills did not miss much in having Lenglen on its courts but a few hours.

Overshadowed by Lenglen and dissatisfied to have beaten her by default, Molla Mallory went on to win the 1921 championship, just as she had done in 1915, 1916, 1917, 1918 and 1920. She held the cup two more years, winning her seventh title in 1926. Not even Wills ever matched this record. Yet Mallory was never quite in the Wills class after beating her in the finals at Forest Hills in 1922 6–3, 6–1. She herself knew that she had but one great stroke, a masterful forehand, and she never took tennis as seriously as most champions do. It took Tilden, that tennis scholar, to point out to her that she had tremendous top spin on her forehand, which al-

Molla Bjurstedt Mallory is beating May Sutton Bundy (near court) in the 1921 semifinals at Forest Hills.

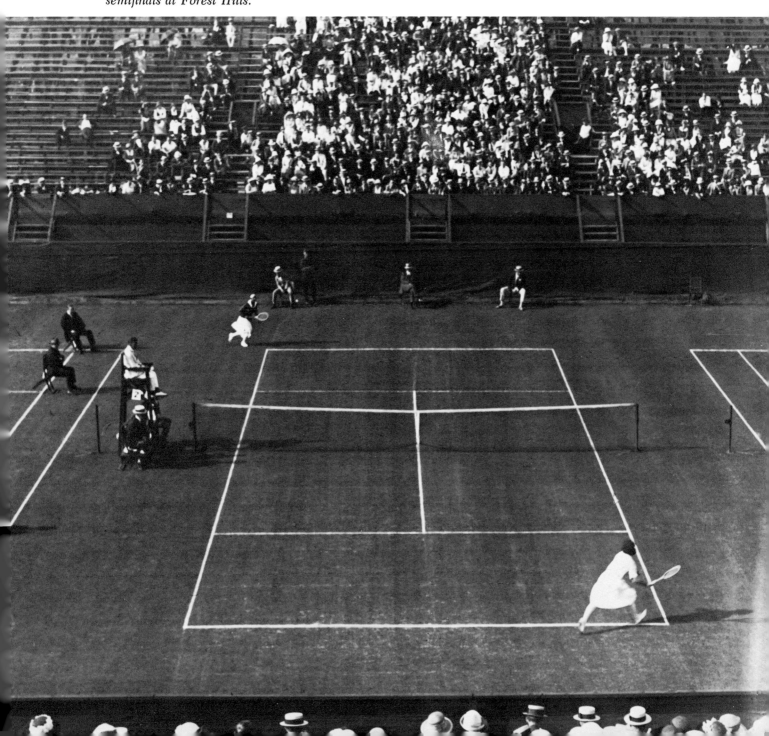

Suzanne Lenglen, the greatest player of the twenties, better even than Wills, flopped badly when she came to Forest Hills in 1921.

lowed her to wallop the ball with her masseuse arm and still keep it in the court. (The aerodynamics of top spin is that a slight vacuum under the front of the spinning ball allows air pressure to force it downward. Almost every instructor will try to get his pupils to stroke the ball as if stroking a cat, bringing the strings upward across the ball and imparting the spin that will keep the shot in the court. Laver can loop shot after shot onto or within inches of the baseline because of top spin—and years of practice!)

After Molla married a wealthy stockbroker in 1919, she let his social calendar determine her way of life and she neither trained nor practiced often. Still, she was the best of the American women until Wills, beating Wightman, Browne, Goss and Zinderstein, the top competition at home. Abroad she was almost as much of a flop as Lenglen was in America, and this was hard for her to realize. Her first set against Lenglen had convinced her that she was the better of the pair, which simply was not true. It was the difference between a good player and a very great player. And America wanted a very great player. The public had tired of Molla, knowing that she was inferior to the best British players and to Lenglen.

Helen Wills appeared just at the right time to become queen of the courts.

"In Miss Wills' game . . . there are the possibilities of future championships," a prophetic sportswriter observed in the summer of 1922. She lost to Mallory in the singles at Forest Hills but won the doubles championship with Marion Zinderstein Jessup.

Only 2,500 were in the stands at Forest Hills for those events. The

Helen Wills, Tilden's female counterpart, beat everyone but Lenglen. She won seven titles and dominated the game for a decade.

ladies just were not drawing. Had it not been for the Davis Cup, Forest Hills would have been a mighty empty place. The West Side Tennis Club was not content to let the men's championships rotate. After all, it had begun as a men's club and there were restrictions on the number of women who could belong and on the hours women could use the courts.

An attempt to put women on an equal footing had been defeated earlier in 1922, even after the women offered to pay the same dues. The men wanted the courts weekends and after 4 P.M., the hours when they were free to play. To this day women's memberships are limited to 165, plus 43 girls, out of a total of 690 active members, and women have no vote at club meetings.

But it could be said that women were the inspiration for the idea of building a stadium, since in 1922 Wimbledon put up a stadium in anticipation of the crowds coming to see Lenglen play. Knowing then that 14,000 people could be comfortably seated in a permanent stadium, considering the cost of installing grandstands every year and, more important, considering that the grandstands were set up on courts and thereby restricted members' playing during tournaments, the West Side's Board of Governors began to investigate the feasibility of putting up a concrete structure—like the Yale Bowl but on a much smaller scale.

But how could such an undertaking be economically justified with the men's nationals in Philadelphia and the women not pulling in spectators? Once again it was the Davis Cup that made Forest Hills the center of the tennis universe in 1921–1923.

11

THE CHALLENGE ROUND
AND THE STADIUM

IT IS HARD TODAY TO REALIZE how significant the Davis Cup used to be. After World War I an atmosphere of international good fellowship took hold for a time and the Davis Cup acquired a significance it lacked in its beginnings and lacks now. It began as an affair between Great Britain and its former colonies, and gradually included Belgium, France, Australia and Germany. In 1921 eleven countries competed and a few years later the number doubled. Today over fifty countries play each other, but in the United States the cup excites limited interest. No Davis Cup matches have been played at Forest Hills since 1959. The USLTA has chosen to rotate these matches among a number of cities.

In the twenties it was a different story, in part because of the phenomenal success of the American teams that kept the Davis Cup in this country for seven straight years. During only three of these years the challenge round took place at Forest Hills, but, as in 1914, they were tremendous matches and they served to reinforce the West Side Club's hold over major events during a period when the men's singles championships were held in Philadelphia. The Davis Cup was front-page news, and when Tilden threatened to quit the team because he had been accused of professionalism, a national calamity was feared.

The first competition the United States entered after 1914 was in 1920. Tilden and Johnston sailed to Australia, wiped out Brookes and Patterson in singles and doubles, and brought the cup to New York like war heroes. This meant that the next challenge round would be played in America, and the West Side Club was very happy to let Philadelphia have the men's nationals for a change while the USLTA awarded New York the real plum —the Davis Cup. It is a lot easier to stage five matches in a three-day period than to put on a tournament with 128 competitors playing matches out for a week or more. As of 1921 Forest Hills has also had the ladies' national championships, but this is a less burdensome tournament because only half as many players are involved.

The 1921 matches with Japan were a sellout. A crowd of 14,000 came daily, Forest Hills' biggest attendance to date. Tilden and Johnston won their singles from Kumagae and Shimizu, who were beaten in the doubles by Williams and Washburn. A clean sweep again, and the Americans kept the cup, as they would for another five years, during their greatest period of tennis ascendancy. Shimizu forced Tilden to five sets in terrible heat and humidity. Down two sets to one, Tilden was so exhausted that he stepped into the shower with his clothes on for eight minutes, and then got Sam Hardy, the Davis Cup captain, to remove the soggy garments and dress him. Shimizu sat on the clubhouse porch without changing, and his failure to put on fresh clothes may have caused the cramps he developed in the fifth set. Suzanne Lenglen in one of her articles expressed amazement at Tilden's recovery of form in the nationals at Philadelphia. She had yet to realize that Tilden could always play cliff-hanging matches in which he looked erratic and sloppy. Five-set matches were his specialty.

The nature of the crowd seemed to be changing. Instead of reporting the names of boxholders who were socially prominent, the West Side Club sent out a list of notables attending the Davis Cup matches—that is, tennis notables, players, organizers and supporters of the game. The Newport image was fading as the game became a national undertaking of real importance. Louis Graves, a member of the West Side, in reviewing Tilden's book *The Art of Lawn Tennis*, remarked that there is little literature on tennis (as opposed to instructional manuals) because it is so "immaculate, correct and singularly devoid of atmosphere. . . . There is little humor in the game." He called tennis "the most enthralling and least whimsical of games."

As tennis grew more serious, it became more popular and more involved in big money. The 1921 Davis Cup gate for three days was $79,000, and the profits of $32,650 were shared by the two countries. At Germantown the nationals, even with local hero Tilden winning, drew only 14,000 for the entire week, with both gate and profits lower than those of the Davis Cup. The ladies' singles drew 10,250 at Forest Hills, with a gate of $22,916. In letting the men's singles rotate without protest, the West Side Tennis Club had managed to come off with more money and more attention than the Germantown Cricket Club.

It was no wonder that in the USLTA meeting a few months later the idea of rotating the biggest events was questioned on the grounds that the association ought to schedule them wherever there was more income to be earned. The West Side's capacity for bringing in the money was not lost on the public when the club announced it had appropriated $30,000 to expand the clubhouse further.

The 1922 Davis Cup matches at Forest Hills saw the Americans triumph over Australia again, but for the first time in three years the U.S.A. lost the doubles and the score was four matches to one. The same players, Tilden and Richards, who had beaten the Australian team of Patterson and Wood in the national doubles at Longwood, lost in straight sets at Forest Hills. The Davis Cup Committee was disappointed. The spirit of competition was so high that the team was expected to sweep every challenge round. Next year, they resolved, things would be different.

During the presentation ceremonies Gerald Patterson gave a speech of thanks for the courtesy of the crowd. It was not intended to be pointed, but everyone knew how boorishly partisan the crowds had been recently in Boston and Philadelphia. World Team Tennis did not introduce noise to tennis spectators; it simply validated an old practice and extended its application. At least Forest Hills got the reputation for having unprejudiced spectators.

The continuing success of the Davis Cup matches was the clincher in the question of building a stadium at Forest Hills and thereby recapturing the men's nationals from Philadelphia. The club's plans to build were announced publicly even before the means to pay for the undertaking had been found. Two members, former president Charles Landers, an engineer, and Kenneth M. Murchison, an architect, drew up plans for a 14,000-seat horseshoe stadium to be built on additional land that would be acquired from the Sage Foundation.

The USLTA was shown the plans and asked how a deal might be worked out to finance the $150,000 project. Obviously the club would have to be guaranteed against the rotation of major events in order to secure the income for the country's only tennis stadium. On January 20, 1923, the press reported that the stadium would be completed during the summer and said it would represent to the United States what Wimbledon does to England. Two weeks later the USLTA explained the following deal: A ten-year contract had been drawn guaranteeing the West Side Club the 1923 Davis Cup challenge round; the men's national singles from 1924 to 1928; the men's singles, Davis Cup or men's national doubles from 1929 to 1932. This made it possible to sell in advance 1,500 box seats for five years at $100 each, providing the money to pay for the capital outlay to build the stadium. After 1932 the USLTA would award the big events on the basis of the best financial offer. What other club could beat Forest Hills once it got a stadium? To the present moment none has found it economically feasible to build a stadium exclusively for tennis matches played a few weeks of the year.

The USLTA projected a $100,000 profit to the West Side Club after taxes and $320,000 income for itself from the stadium during the next ten years. With this kind of money at its disposal the USLTA could then give strong support to the 265 tournaments it was scheduling annually. Forest Hills, in other words, was making it possible for the USLTA to promote tennis and regulate its tournaments and rankings with even more authority than heretofore. The USLTA's marriage to Forest Hills was a marriage of convenience that has outlasted the marriage of love, which ended in divorce when Newport was disenfranchised in 1915.

The West Side, as usual, once having made its decision, moved rapidly. In this day and age of strikes and shortages it hardly seems possible that a stadium could be built in a few months. Construction began April 9 and was sufficiently completed by August for the irrepressible Julian Myrick to stage a special event for a grand opening. He had been succeeded in the presidency of the USLTA by Dwight Davis, father of the Davis Cup, and was again free to devote his energies to promoting the interests of the West Side Club. Lying fallow in that alert brain of his was a proposal by one of the great ladies of tennis, Hazel Hotchkiss Wightman, a Californian transplanted to Boston. More than two years had gone by since the USLTA had tabled her offer to provide a cup for international ladies' matches. Male chauvinism would not welcome a rival to the Davis Cup.

On his own initiative Myrick proceeded to wire Mrs. Wightman that the club was prepared to launch her international series of team matches in the new stadium. As with the Davis Cup, they would begin with Great Britain and, they hoped, expand to include other countries (a hope that was never fulfilled).

Hazel Wightman had won the singles and doubles titles for three years, 1909 to 1911, and the doubles in 1915, and before she put down her racket at the age of sixty-eight she had won a grand total of fourteen national titles. She probably did more for women's tennis than anyone, including Billie Jean King. It was characteristic of her to respond positively to Myrick's invitation and she quickly put together a team of Mallory, Wills and Goss to play in five singles and two doubles matches (in contrast to the Davis Cup's four singles and one doubles). The winner had to win four matches. Like Davis, Mrs. Wightman bought a silver cup in Boston for presentation to the winning team.

The stadium was not quite completed, but there was ample room for the 5,000 who came to the opening on August 10. They were pleased with what they saw initially, an open bowl to seat 14,000, 195 feet long and 145 feet wide, with room for three courts—in contrast to Wimbledon's single court. A 10-foot concrete wall provided a good background for seeing the ball, and with the spectators sitting above this barrier their movements and colors would not distract the players. The thirty-nine rows of seats broken by ten entrances rose to a height of 51 feet at the top, where there was a 715-foot promenade and a fine view of the field of turf stretching to the clubhouse.

Hazel Hotchkiss Wightman, who conceived the Wightman Cup matches between British and American women's teams, continued to wield a racket almost to the day she died, at the age of eighty-seven.

Action during the famous match that Wills (way back) defaulted to an aggressive Jacobs, seen slamming an overhead.

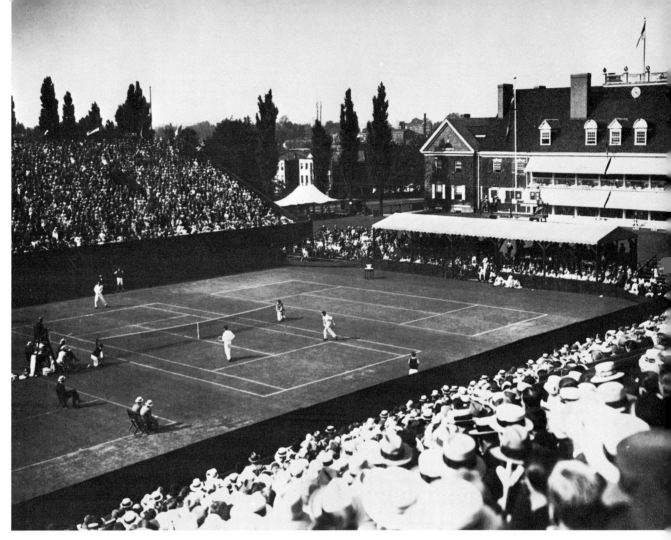

At Germantown Cricket Club in 1925, Lacoste and Borotra, of France, are losing to Richards and Williams.

Forest Hills packs them in for the 1922 Davis Cup, which gleams in the center of the unused court, while Tilden smacks a forehand at Australia's Gerald Patterson.

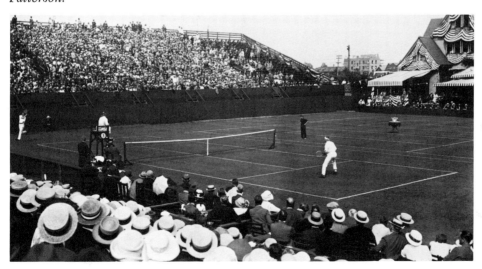

111

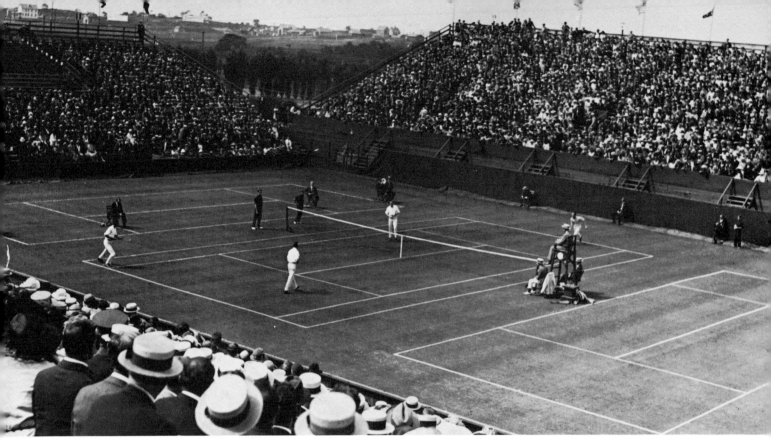

Tilden and his protégé Richards (near court) go down in straight sets to the Australians Patterson and Wood in the 1922 Davis Cup matches.

An aerial view of Wimbledon in the twenties reveals it as a model of what Forest Hills was striving for: the village architecture, the triangular shape of the grounds. Wimbledon is far more spacious, though now urbanized.

At the open end a raised marquee covered with an awning provided a place for players, officials, the press and a few hundred selected spectators. Its discreetness made a convenient "wing," as in a theater, from which players could make a ritualistic entrance, walking down ten brick steps with several rackets under their arms.

Almost nothing has changed in that scene since 1923. Boxes have been added in front of the closed end of the horseshoe, and the south concrete wall has been replaced with an ingenious one-way plastic screen that allows people sitting in the Open Club under the Stadium to watch matches at ground level (a bit like watching them underwater). The players cannot see through the screen into the Open Club.

Billie Jean King complained in her book, *Billie Jean* (1974), that the background of the Stadium, being slightly curved because of the horseshoe shape, is a bit hard to get used to, but no other player has said anything about it, and it has not kept Billie Jean from winning titles. Putting aside the question of the quality of the grass, which was not all that bad because the three courts were used in rotation, the West Side Stadium offers optimum conditions for player and spectator alike. Compare it with the Grandstand outside the north end of the Stadium. Here wind, noise and the general lack of cozy seclusion make for a much less desirable tennis, and it was this sort of setup, though on a larger scale, that existed prior to 1923.

A ceremony including four trumpeters on top of the promenade, the playing of "The Star-Spangled Banner," and the hoisting of British and American flags as well as the club flag preceded the first match between Helen Wills and the British star Kathleen McKane. The arena was christened the West Side Stadium, but it is often referred to as Forest Hills Stadium.

Wills won her match 6–2, 7–5, and the Americans swept the series, Mrs. Wightman playing doubles with Eleanor Goss. In fifty-one years of playing alternately in England and the United States, England has won the Wightman Cup only eleven times. The matches have been played at Forest Hills ten times, the last being in 1974. Despite Mrs. Wightman's belief that professionals should be kept off the teams, this proved impossible, and like the Davis Cup teams, the Wightman Cup teams are now chosen from among the best players, pro or amateur. The Wightman Cup series, however, probably embodies more than any event in tennis the early spirit of sportsmanship and international goodwill.

Until she died in 1974 at the age of eighty-eight, Mrs. Wightman lived in the Brookline, Massachusetts, home where so many visiting players at Longwood had known her hospitality. When the British sportswriter Laurie Pignon visited her in 1973, after she had been named a Commander of the British Empire by the Queen of England, she took him to her garage, where she had helped dozens of players improve their game, handed him a racket and showed him how to relax and hit the ball with an unhurried stroke. She cured Helen Wills's clumsy footwork by making her walk up

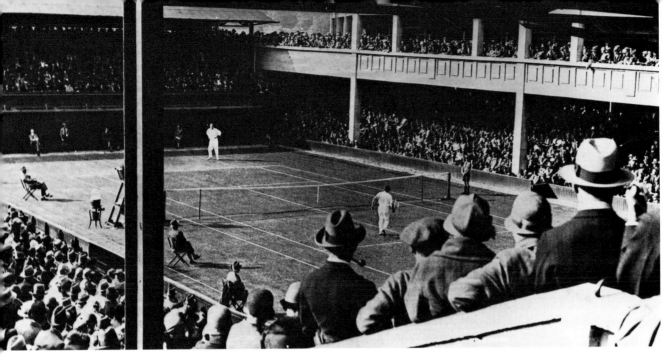

Wimbledon's Court Number One, backed up against the oval stadium housing the famous Centre Court. The man about to smash a short lob is Borotra. The ball boy is a boy scout.

and down stairs, and then teamed with her to win the doubles championship at Wimbledon in 1924.

Helen Wills's surprisingly easy victory over Kathleen McKane was the stage setter for her match a few days later in the finals of the national singles championship against thirty-seven-year-old Molla Mallory. Before 6,000 people in the Stadium this silent, unsmiling girl of seventeen in the white eyeshade demolished the aging champion in thirty-three minutes, 6–2, 6–1. It was the end of a long reign and the beginning of the reign of Queen Helen. Molla had been *the* figure for ten years, winning seven titles, and she was to win one more at the age of forty, when Helen Wills had to default because of an attack of appendicitis.

Wills, a California girl trained partly by her father and more by a coach named William "Pop" Fuller, modeled her game after the hard-hitting McLoughlin and played with men to give her stiff competition. She was described in that first finals as an Amazon. She was also known as Miss Poker Face because of her capacity to conceal her feelings. This mask was undoubtedly to protect herself against the potential volatility she knew was within her, and on rare occasions it showed. Few women weep when they lose. They are more likely to smile and congratulate the winner. Lenglen wept and so did Wills, after a three-set loss in 1924 to McKane in a Wightman Cup match. Like Lenglen, Helen Wills found losing a traumatic experience. An unpopular quality at times, but it makes champions. The fact that Wills was a grim-visaged competitor did not keep the galleries from filling up to watch her play.

With a new stadium and a new star to fill it along with Tilden, Forest Hills was now in a position to offer the greatest tennis America had ever seen, season after season.

12

CONFRONTING
COMMERCIALISM

Following the victory of Helen Wills in 1923 there was a Davis Cup match at Forest Hills with Australia which the United States won 4–1. But this victory caused more headaches than defeat might have. The only loss came on the first day when Anderson beat Johnston in five sets. Tilden won his match over Patterson in straight sets to even the score. Thus winning the doubles became rather critical. Tilden and Richards had lost the doubles the year before, so the committee picked Williams to be Tilden's partner.

The first set of the doubles proved to be the longest in Davis Cup history up to that point, lasting from 2:40 to 5:50. A crowd of 10,000 in the Stadium watched the Americans finally take it 17–15. But the second set went against them 11–13 and they dropped the third 3–6. Tilden was playing badly, not taking the net much, and when he did, volleying weakly. Down two sets to one, the Americans went into the clubhouse to shower and change. While they were dressing the chairman of the Davis Cup Committee of the USLTA, Harold Hackett, offered Tilden some un-asked-for advice on how to win the match. It boiled down to: "Bill, you've got to get up to the net."

Bill did not like criticism and he replied ungraciously and stalked off to the Stadium in a rage. But it was quickly noticed that something new had been added to his game. For one thing the Americans had switched sides with each other so that Tilden stood where he preferred, in the right-hand court. And he played in close to the net. They won easily, 6–3, 6–2. Tilden was acclaimed for his recovery and went down to Philadelphia, where he creamed Johnston so badly in the finals that it was over in less than an hour. *The New York Times* in an editorial declared him to be a "genius with a racket much as Kreisler is with a bow." At thirty Tilden had had his most successful season, and belonged with Ruth, Dempsey and Jones as one of the athletes of the age.

But what was Tilden to do with all this energy when the competitions were over? He was unmarried. His own family had all died before he was twenty-one. He was a loner, admired but too waspish and cold to have many close friends. One avocation was the stage, to which he had become attracted while summering in the Catskills. A few turns on Broadway convinced the world at large that he did his best acting being himself and nobody else, but he continued his occasional sallies into the theater, one as late as 1942. He even considered a career in Hollywood, but he was not a trouper. His other avocation was writing, and at this he was successful. He wrote boys' tennis fiction, he wrote excellent books on the game, some of the best ever written, and he wrote by-line articles for newspapers and magazines. He had no need for a ghostwriter.

No sooner was the season over in 1923 than an article by Tilden appeared in *American Lawn Tennis*, a monthly of small circulation published by the USLTA, in which he took a swipe at the Davis Cup Committee, saying the time to issue instructions was not between the third and fourth sets. He had not forgotten Hackett's gratuitous admonition in the West Side locker room, and it turned out that Hackett had not forgotten the first two sets Tilden's poor play had lost. Two months passed and in the November issue of *American Lawn Tennis* there appeared a letter from Hackett replying to Tilden's affrontery. This letter set off a chain reaction that nearly blew Tilden out of amateur tennis and eventually required the weighty influence of the West Side Club, to which Hackett had belonged for a generation, to keep the master from retiring.

Anyone who has ever talked to ex-champions knows what powerful and sensitive people they are as far as tennis is concerned. To be a champion is to be single-minded and to concentrate with such force on each point that it is forever engraved on the mind. Ask any great player to recall a match, and thirty years later he can vividly reconstruct point after point. Hackett had held the national doubles title for four years with Alexander, from 1907 to 1910. Neither player rates any space in Will Grimsley's thorough *Tennis, Its History, People and Events*. But Hackett probably knew doubles strategy as well as anyone, and Tilden was not a finished doubles player. Instead of taking up the matter privately with Tilden, who was now a leading public figure, Hackett self-indulgently, in the manner of a patriarch, wrote to the editor of *American Lawn Tennis* a very intemperate letter that was immediately reproduced in the daily papers.

Calling him the greatest tennis player of all time, Hackett wrote that Tilden "absolutely fails to understand the great fundamental of the doubles game, which is position play." He self-righteously pointed out the committee's responsibility for the Davis Cup as akin to that of a coach who gets the blame for losses, and explained how they pondered the choice of Tilden for the doubles. Although Tilden had been national doubles champion in 1922, his playing in the Davis Cup, according to Hackett, had been "atrocious" that year. Yet he was chosen again in 1923. "That he chose to park his intelligence outside the stadium naturally was entirely unexpected by the committee," Hackett wrote. However, between the third and fourth set the committee told Tilden what to do, and (thanks to the committee) he redeemed what had been to Hackett the poorest doubles exhibition since the cup was donated in 1900. Concluding this patronizing screed, Hackett suggested Tilden find a doubles partner to play with consistently and work on his doubles game for a season.

The Davis Cup was displayed in the drawing room of the West Side Tennis Club amid an imitation Tudor decor.

A rare picture of Julian Myrick, one of the most influential organizers of amateur tennis.

Well! If Bill Talbert were to publish something like this about Stan Smith after losing in the doubles against Rumania in 1971, even the mild-mannered Smith might have sounded off. But mildness was not in Tilden's makeup. He was a man of extremes, bordering on irrationality at times and loss of control. He nearly got into a fist fight once just watching a match. He could be as tough an opponent off the court as on, and in the five-set style he did not mind dragging a controversy on for months.

The day after the Hackett letter hit the papers, December 5, 1923, Tilden issued a statement denouncing the Davis Cup Committee, saying that he would not play for the team again and that the USLTA would be asked to look into the way its Davis Cup Committee operated. "I am disgusted with the star-chamber methods of the committee," he said.

In a sudden rush of modesty Tilden stated that he did not consider himself a first-class doubles player and had not even expected to play the doubles in 1923. The committee, he claimed, gave him only thirty-six hours' notice, so how could he and Williams have worked out a strategy? With some justice he wondered what Hackett was so upset about, since they had won the match, and he particularly resented the insult about his intelligence. Why had the committee not given the team some instructions *before* the match? He reiterated that the locker-room advice was useless. What happened was that he changed sides with Williams, changed his spikes* and played harder because he was "more desperate." Deploring the secrecy of the committee, he dug up ancient history: McLoughlin and Bundy had been given very little notice in 1914 that they would play together, and they lost.

He had something of a point. Clifford Sutter, who had ranked third and fourth in 1932 and 1933, was told in 1934 to "wait" until the committee made a decision. He had to wait in New York at his own expense and was finally denied a place on a Davis Cup team that lost to Great Britain. He was never told why he was not chosen, and the decision may have cost America the cup.

The *New York Times* editorial entitled "Temperamental Tennis" good-humoredly praised the professionals for being less sensitive than the amateurs:

> When Mr. Ruth stepped up to the plate in the 8th inning with the bases full and his team one run behind and Mr. Huggins ordered him to take two, he took two, even though he struck out in consequence. . . . With all reverent genuflection before the amateur spirit one still feels that there is a discipline in professional sports which trains men to stand the gaff.

Criticism was not the point, however. The issue was amateurism and its definition. And the beat went on as the USLTA in January expressed alarm

119

* The last year for spikes at Forest Hills was 1923. They were ruled out after crepe-soled tennis shoes were developed. On exceptionally slippery days, however, they were permitted for many years after the ban.

over the growth of commercialism and professionalism. They certainly had the problem analyzed:

> Tennis has become so popular, the competition for supremacy so keen and the desire of the players to improve their game so strong that some players have not realized that there is this very serious problem to be faced.

The problem was how a player could play enough to compete and have time enough to hold a job. The USLTA perspective was that of middle-aged men of means who had played competitively but had not faced the consistent quality of competition that was developing in the twenties. They suggested that players should either be businessmen or have a profession. What was particularly wrong by USLTA lights was for a tennis player to make a living from articles that newspapers paid big sums for because the name players' by-lines pulled in circulation.

Tilden immediately replied in the most disingenuous manner imaginable. He told reporters that the USLTA could not have been thinking of him because he was a writer before he was a tennis player and traced his suddenly discovered profession back to his college days! A month later the USLTA officially banned article writing by the players as of January 1, 1925, and they did so by the overwhelming vote of 47,186 to 6,250, the bulk, of course, being proxies. At the same time they ruled that players' expenses must be paid through clubs and not by individuals. Tilden was notorious for running up heavy expense accounts which were gladly covered by wealthy patrons.

The exchanges with Tilden were like deep lobs and took time to be returned. Tilden came back thirty days after the USLTA policy announcement during an after-dinner speech in Hartford in which he said he would quit the Davis Cup if the USLTA enforced the writing ban. And a week later he did withdraw voluntarily from the Olympic team, which was playing in Paris that summer, on the grounds that his writing made him a pro by Olympic standards. However, he allowed his name to be drawn for the Davis Cup matches conducted by President Coolidge on the White House lawn before assembled diplomats. The Davis Cup, said Tilden, meant a great deal more than the Olympics. He added that "writing comes first" and that he would give up tennis January 1 if necessary.

It was getting to be spring, and in mid-April Tilden suddenly sent a letter of resignation to the USLTA saying that "to save the committee embarrassment" he would not play on the Davis Cup team. Julian Myrick as a spokesman expressed surprise, since Tilden had not been censured by the committee, and urged Tilden if he meant it to be consistent and not play in amateur tournaments. The seriousness of the possibility of losing Tilden altogether at the height of his career drew an editorial supporting the great player in *The New York Times*. It spoke of the "increasing complexity of amateur" tennis, and defended Tilden's writing as the real thing and not ghostwritten material.

On May 6, 1924, a group of forty members of the West Side Tennis Club met at the Hotel Vanderbilt to voice opposition to the USLTA's ban on writing articles as an unwarrantedly strict interpretation of the rules governing amateurism. But the club membership as a whole went with the USLTA at a special meeting on May 15 by a vote of 181–155. The press noted that a large element of the most powerful club in the country was afraid of a fall in gate receipts if Tilden dropped out of tennis.

So that was how the off-season was passed, endlessly debating in public whether you can be a little bit pregnant. Of course Tilden did hold the trump card. The public uproar if he had really gone through with his threat would have been too much for the USLTA. On June 6 the USLTA caved. Very quietly a compromise was reached, but no one was ever told what it was. Tilden agreed to play on the Davis Cup team. The USLTA had no comment whatsoever. One can only surmise that the compromise consisted of a cease-fire on both sides. Tilden continued to write but he kept his mouth shut. And Forest Hills got its gate.

However, four years later hostilities broke out once again over the very same issue, and this time, after Tilden wrote a newspaper article on Wimbledon while he was playing there, the USLTA, at the urging of Tilden's enemies, barred him from tournaments and from Davis Cup competition in France in 1928. Now it was the French who had to worry about the gate! The issue was important enough to take to the American ambassador, Myron Herrick, who cabled Washington that the USLTA was damaging international relations. Thus Tilden briefly became part of American foreign policy. State Department pressure was brought on the authorities in New York, and Tilden was reinstated.

Tilden did not let his country down and played what George Lott said was his greatest match of all time in the new Roland Garros Stadium in Paris on clay against Lacoste, an overwhelming favorite. He beat the Frenchman, in five sets, for the only American victory in the series. He was on the decline, and three years later at the age of thirty-eight he turned pro. That was the difference in the days of shamateurism. You clung to your amateur standing, picking up what pin money you could, and then, when you were no longer a champion, you went on tour. Now, if you are any good at all you become a pro before you are twenty-one. It's the only way to find the time to make a living and keep up with the competition on the court.

13

THE FRENCH CONNECT

TILDEN AND WILLS *were* Forest Hills in 1924 and 1925. The Battle of the Bills continued, with Johnston finally going down in straight sets in the 1924 finals but almost beating Tilden in 1925 in five.

The way Tilden beat Johnston was to take the pace off Johnston's formidable forehand with slice drives from either side. He believed that Johnston's Western grip tired his arm and that he could always eventually wear him down.

Incidentally, in 1922 Tilden got an infection that required the removal of the first joint of the middle finger on his right hand. Why didn't this affect his own grip and tire his hand? Because Tilden changed the style of his game; instead of engaging in long rallies, he "hit for the winner at once," as he put it. He was always compensating for weaknesses.

Johnston was the "good guy" of tennis and a great player who had the misfortune to come up against one even greater and thus was denied the championship five times. Always good-humored, a strict adherent to the amateur rules and never a show-off, he was a model of classic restraint. His qualities made Tilden's faults all the more glaring. He would never, as Tilden once did, tell the chairman of the tournament at the Orange Lawn Tennis Club that he was not used to playing in a cow pasture.

Perhaps Tilden knew at heart that he was unable to control his own childish petulance and for that reason secretly wished that he had Johnston's decorum. His admiration for the little bantam was deeply felt, and he was grieved by the Californian's premature death from tuberculosis. In 1948 he dedicated his memoirs to "William M. Johnston in everlasting admiration."

After losing to Tilden, Johnston was asked to comment on the fact that Tilden had been beaten that year by Borotra and Lacoste in indoor matches, his first international losses. "He's been spending too much time on the stage, that's all. Tilden is not slipping."

Perhaps not. But Borotra and Lacoste were new names to reckon with. Together with Brugnon and Cochet, they made up the famous Four Musketeers. It is essential to remember how shattered France was by the war. It had lost 1,320,000 military men and 250,000 civilians (the United States lost 53,513 military men), and the franc was worth a fifth of its pre-war value. Still, something like a Roaring Twenties spirit grew out of the elation at driving the Germans off their soil, and enormous national pride was taken in excelling in literature, fashions, food and sports. The Four Musketeers were more than tennis players; they were the embodiment of France itself.

Borotra was the standout at first. Arriving in New York in March 1925, he won the national indoor championship, while Lacoste stayed home to win the French hard-courts. There was no publicity buildup after the Lenglen fiasco, and the French Davis Cup captain, acting like a football coach, deprecated his team by predicting it would not win the cup for five years. And that seemed sensible, for Tilden would then be thirty-seven. Among the tournaments Tilden won in 1925 were the Heights Casino indoor, Buffalo invitation, Florida, Southeastern, New England, Penn State, Metropolitan. He lost to Richards in the finals at Orange.

But Lacoste took Wimbledon, beating Borotra, and the American Davis Cup team was chosen in August only after three days of trial matches at Forest Hills. The Stadium was more frequently used at the outset than it is today. After the trials there in 1925 came two days of East–West matches. The Davis Cup challenge round was played at Germantown, and the vaunted French succumbed 0–5, chiefly because of insufficient experience on the courts. Both Lacoste and Borotra carried Tilden to five sets. Borotra, the older player, was slowing down slightly.

Jean Borotra, a Basque, came from Biarritz, close to the Spanish border. His style of play was crude but dynamic, and it earned him the nickname of the Bounding Basque in the British papers. He wore a beret and was as much of an actor on the courts as Tilden. One trick was to feign exhaustion. He would stagger and appear near death. Vinnie Richards was once taken in by the act and lulled into a false sense of security that cost him the match.

Jean René Lacoste had a private income to support his passion for tennis, and though he may have lacked the natural talent of Borotra and

Cochet, the latter having been considered the most gifted player who ever stepped on a court (Nastase might challenge that), his methodical practice paid off. With the help of his father's automobile factory, he constructed a machine that would toss balls at him from across the court. His tenacity was symbolized by the crocodile which he turned into a highly profitable trademark on sports clothes.

In 1926 these two Frenchmen and Henri Cochet and Jacques Brugnon again challenged for the Davis Cup at Philadelphia and lost 4–1. But the singles win was a five-set victory for Lacoste over Tilden—"an ominous note," Will Grimsley called it. Tilden thereafter considered Lacoste his greatest rival, not Johnston, because he could find no weakness in a game that appeared unflashy. The fact was that Tilden's old knee injury had returned, but he never complained or made excuses when he lost. The following week at Forest Hills he fell victim to Henri Cochet because he could not run well enough and was, in Allison Danzig's phrase, "like Hercules shorn of his power."

A crowd of 9,000 rooted and cheered for Big Bill as he pulled up to 4–4 in the fifth set after a sensational series of volleys. Tilden was never really comfortable at the net, and after that surge he more frequently dropped back to the baseline—drooped back might be more accurate—and Cochet took it 8–6. Cochet at twenty-four looked as good as his two illustrious fellow countrymen. He was a short man of lightning reflexes who often eschewed the space behind the baseline because of his uncanny ability with a shot that is rarely an offensive stroke, the half volley.

On that same day Johnston fell to Borotra, and Williams to Lacoste. Only Brugnon, the fourth musketeer, who specialized in doubles, was beaten—by Richards in straight sets. Forest Hills was shortly confronted with the unusual spectacle of a national finals without Americans, something that would only happen again when Perry and Crawford played in 1933, but which became routine beginning in the mid-fifties. Lacoste easily beat his old rival Borotra in straight sets. It was the first time since the Englishman Doherty won in 1903 that the U.S. men's singles championship left the country. The 1926 finals was no contest and therefore a disappointment. The next year, and the last that Lacoste played at Forest Hills, he had to work for his title, even though he beat Tilden in straight sets.

Behind lay an inspiring 3–2 French victory at Philadelphia for the Davis Cup. Tilden had gone down before in four sets. Now Tilden knew that he must win two of the first three sets to beat the Frenchman. With a packed Stadium longing for a Tilden victory—"If there were any French partisans they did not make themselves known," Danzig reported—the master tried to blow his opponent off the courts with his famed cannonball serve, the most important of his strokes. A good serve, he once said, is one you can't return. In the first set he had three set points, led 3–1 in the second and 5–2 in the third.

Toto Brugnon, writing in *Tennis de France* forty years later, vividly recalled the three chances Tilden had to win the first set, leading 7–6,

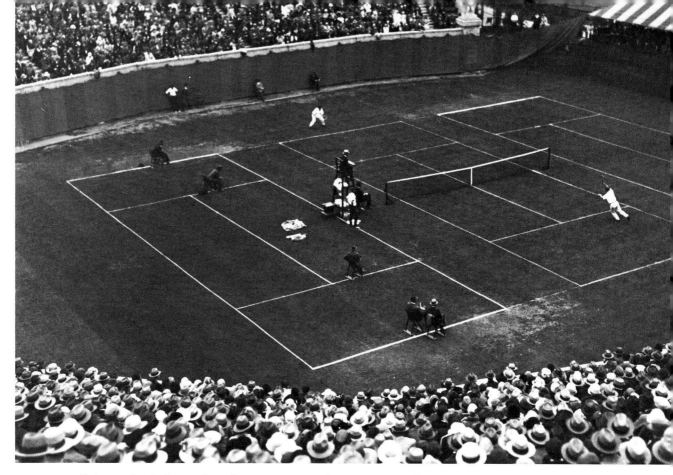

You can tell from the fedoras that the 1926 nationals went on well into September. Vinnie Richards is attacking Jean Borotra (far court)—to no avail.

Quarterfinals, 1926. Tilden serves an American twist to Henri Cochet, the racket finishing to his right. Cochet ended Tilden's reign, but did not win the title himself until 1928.

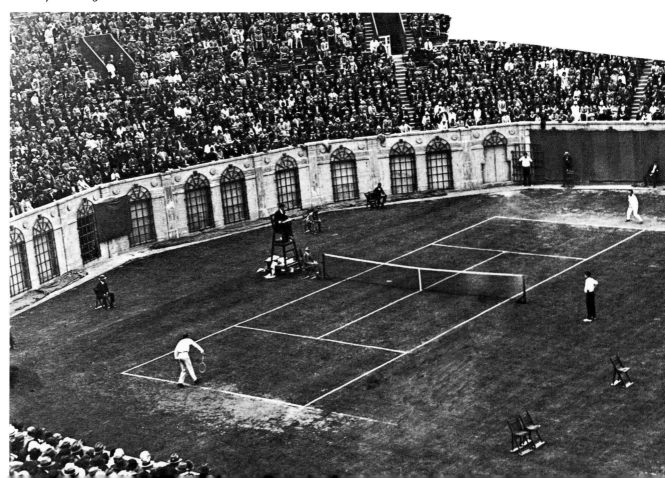

40–love. He could not get that deuce ace, and the reason lay in the disparity of ages between the players. Already Tilden was tiring, and he dropped the first set 11–9. But he would not quit in a match that went on for almost three hours, longer than many five-set matches.

In the second set Tilden charged off with a 4–1 lead, but as Brugnon recalls, "the crocodile clenched his teeth and carried it away 6–4." His strategy against the greatest shotmaker of all time was that of France in the trenches. Lacoste played what is now called percentage tennis, avoiding errors and getting the ball back no matter what. Steadiness has an enormous psychological advantage against a player who knows how spectacular his racket work is. Under the pressure of Lacoste's consistent and tireless returns, which seemed to go deeper and with more pace than he had shown at Germantown, Tilden eventually fell into a series of fatal errors.

While Lacoste was acknowledged a great tennis player, he was not an American crowd pleaser, and in defeat Tilden took that huge throng with him. If he had just put over one cannonball in the first set—if, if, if. A spectator remarked that he had seen the greatest tennis match of all and nothing would surpass it.

He had also seen the last of Lacoste, who retired the next year. Returning to France with the Davis Cup, the French team was confronted with a situation typical of their customs service: the great silver cup would cost somebody 40,000 francs' duty, said the misinformed man at the Le Havre dock. Official intercession produced a magnanimous *libre entrée*, the duty-free cup was put on display in Paris, and the premier received Lacoste and his teammates at the Elysée Palace.

The French held the cup until the rise of the British in 1933. Cochet beat Hunter for the American title in 1928 (Tilden was suspended by the USLTA and could not enter), and that was it for the French at Forest Hills. It is a curious thing that since 1928, with all de Gaulle's talk of *gloire*, only one French player of note has appeared at Forest Hills. Small countries, such as Rumania and Czechoslovakia, have been able to produce champions on the order of Kodes and Nastase. Françoise Durr, who it was said could never be a first-class player because on the backhand she puts her forefinger on top of the racket handle and not around it, has been a doubles champion at Forest Hills twice—in 1969 with Darlene Hard, and in 1972 with Betty Stove.

14

ERA'S END

THE YEAR 1929 CONVENIENTLY CLOSES the euphoric period that helped to establish Forest Hills as one of the world's great sports centers. It was the last year of speculative prosperity. No longer would Saks Fifth Avenue run full-page ads for "The Well-Dressed Chauffeur 1926–1927," featuring smart uniforms and fur-lined coats at $300 (some limousines had no roof over the front seat, and auto heaters had not been introduced). As if to reassure the world that "normalcy" consisted of no change in the status quo, Tilden came back to win the national singles title for the seventh time, beating Francis T. Hunter in five sets at the age of thirty-six. No man since Larned had been champion this often, and no one ever before or since ranked first ten years in a row.

Only 9,000 came for a match marred by errors. Frank Hunter, an outstanding doubles player from New Rochelle, New York, had won the national doubles championship with Tilden in 1927, and he had beaten an aging Borotra in Holland, but Tilden had won the Eastern championships from him at Rye in straight sets. After beating Doeg in a five-set semifinals at Forest Hills, Hunter was not expected to put up much of a scrap against his old partner. But having lost the previous year's finals to Cochet, he hoped to get his name on the great trophy.

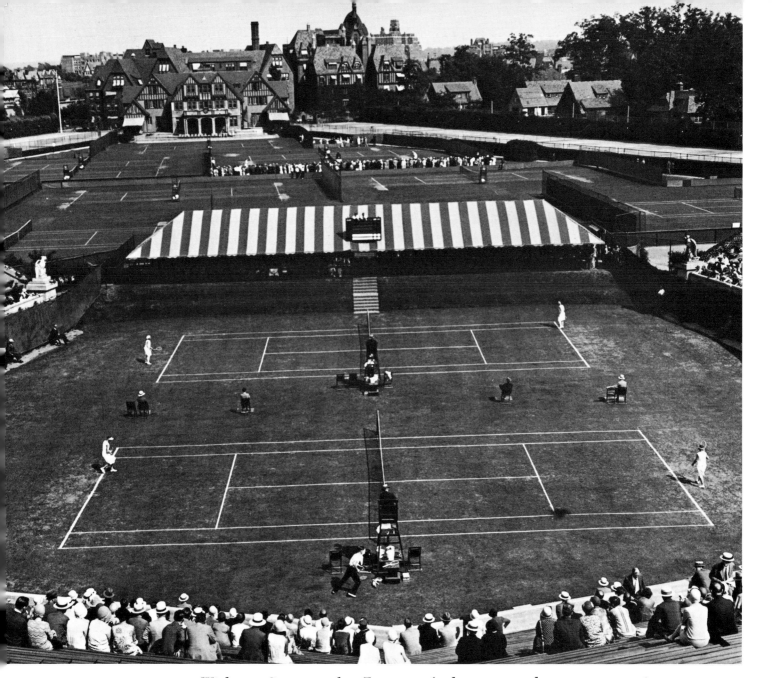

Wightman Cup team play. For want of adequate secondary spectator seating, two matches used to be played in the Stadium at the same time.

Tilden had no knee trouble and retained all the old magic, ending the match with two cannonball serves Hunter could not handle. He then said he would retire from competition, but next season he changed his mind.

Champions do not like to yield their places. Tenacity is what makes them champions–that plus *training*. Tilden said that the hallmark of the champion is the quality of scrambling, the willingness to do anything to keep the ball in play. That means sometimes doing anything to avoid defeat. Number one and still champion, Tilden at thirty-seven played the circuit one more year. He won at Wimbledon, he won the Eastern. Then at Rye in August he ran up against Cliff Sutter, national intercollegiate

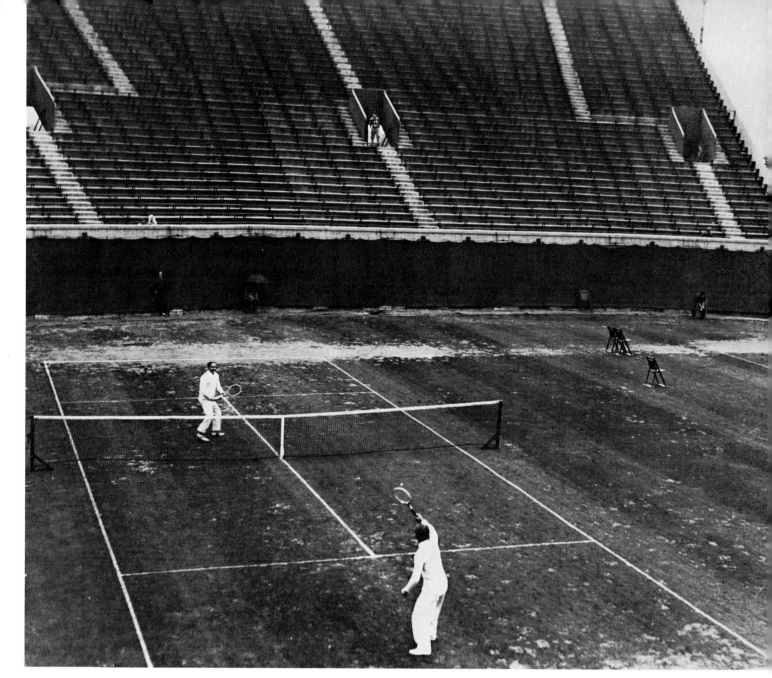

Zero attendance set some kind of record when Karel Kozeluh beat John Collom (facing net) in an early round of the second pro championships in 1933.

champion from Tulane. The nineteen-year-old kid whipped the old man 6–0 in the first set and went ahead 4–1 in the second. Tilden was acting ungracious about the hiding he was getting when he heard a woman in the stands say loudly, "He's a bum sport. Let's get on his nerves."

"Okay," said Tilden, walking rapidly to the umpire, "I default." Sutter and the officials could not kid the ex-champion into continuing the match.

A week later at Newport the two were again paired. Young Sutter could not resist faking a limp when he saw Tilden enter the Casino in street clothes, for the story had developed that the old knee injury had forced him to default at Rye. Other players watching Sutter limp around roared, and Tilden shouted, "I never said it was my knee, Cliff. Come on, let's get dressed and play tennis."

Sutter in recollection says, "Tilden could be difficult but he was very prompt. He never used his position to keep lesser players waiting. We started out from the locker room together and on the way he was hailed by some friends. I kept going and got to the court first. Tilden had the habit, if anyone kept him waiting, of bouncing a ball nervously with his racket endlessly until the opponent showed up. So I began bouncing that ball like mad and Tilden saw me. He took off like a gazelle, leaping over those three-foot screens between courts. When he got to the court he spun his racket and shouted, 'Call it, Cliff!' "

Sutter does not kid himself that he was the equal of Tilden even at that time. They went to five sets and he thought he had worn Tilden out, but experience made the difference and Tilden took the last set 8–6. They never played against each other again.

Tilden as champion had one more national singles tournament to play that same year, 1930, and, seeded one, he advanced to the semifinals losing only one set in the quarterfinals to George Lott, an all-time great doubles player and a fine tennis writer. His opponent was John Doeg, a left-hander with nothing but a serve, but a serve superior even to Tilden's cannonball, which was flat. Doeg's blinding blur of a serve was unusual because it had a terrific spin, which usually slows down the ball. He could pull his opponent five feet off the court and take the net for the put-away. Tilden held on for four sets, losing the first 10–8 and the last 12–10.

Doeg won the finals against Francis X. Shields in four and again needed 10–8 in the first and 16–14 in the fourth. It was Doeg's only singles title. He held the doubles title with Lott in 1929 and 1930. In 1931 he was only seeded fifth at Forest Hills and was eliminated in the semifinals in straight sets by his partner, Lott. The winner of the finals was a lad who only had reached the third round the year before, Ellsworth Vines.

After the 1930 season Tilden decided to turn pro, and made the announcement on December 31. Pro tennis in those days was organized as a series of exhibitions. Pro tournaments were rare. In golf a pro gave lessons and also competed, but the tennis instructor was seldom a star who could give the champions a game. Open golf tournaments had existed from the beginning. Under the strict separation of pro and amateur, tennis was being deprived of the continuing competition of its best players like Richards and, after 1930, Tilden.

To its credit, the USLTA wanted an open tournament. Tilden had urged this, and on November 14, 1929, the association cabled the International Lawn Tennis Federation in Paris suggesting a worldwide open. The English Lawn Tennis Association seconded the motion a month later. But in March of 1930 the ILTF turned thumbs down. How prophetic were Tilden's words: "There will be a growing recognition of the necessity of revising the modern amateur code to meet the present conditions of a commercial age."

Tilden certainly recognized his own commercial value. He packed them in not only at Forest Hills but wherever he played because he knew instinctively that the crowd wanted a drama. "Not even Mlle. Suzanne Lenglen in her white robe tripping across the Forest Hills greensward in 1921," wrote Allison Danzig, "with the eclat of a ballet dancer had a more accentuated sense of the dramatic or a keener faculty for exploiting it, consciously or unconsciously."

To give the crowd its money's worth he would allow a weak player to take two sets and then pull the match out in breathless fashion. He did not mind taking the role of villain because he understood the fascination we all have for the bad guy. But he would not stand for injustice. The arbitrariness of umpires riled him, and the hypocrisy of the defenders of pure amateurism sent him into a rage. The positions he took were right and he knew it. Like a true leader he was not dismayed by exile. After he had been reinstated to amateur status by government intervention, the USLTA really crawled. He had been expelled for writing articles whose ultimate purpose was said to be building circulation for the papers and magazines.

On April 30 the USLTA advertised that its own magazine would carry Tilden's analysis of the Davis Cup prospects. The public was invited to subscribe to this magazine which carried the by-line of "one of the greatest internationalists of all time." Talk of circulation building!

And Forest Hills, too, was not yet done with Big Bill. In July of 1931, a grim Depression year when a moratorium of international debts had been declared, 4,000 showed up at West Side Stadium for a match that had never been played there in all the years of competition between Tilden and his maturing protégé, Richards. It was the finals of the national pro championships, which forty-four players entered, including Hunter and Kozeluh. If there was any purse, the amount was never announced. These players were playing for fun and for publicity. The press referred to the tournament's sentimental appeal.

Tilden wrote a syndicated column for the North American Newspaper Alliance analyzing the matches, picking Kozeluh over Hunter in four sets (he was right). When Richards beat Kozeluh, Tilden wrote, "I have seldom seen Richards serve better . . . it was one of the finest exhibitions of sustained attack I have ever witnessed." It became his destiny to face this whirlwind in the finals.

Allison Danzig, who had been watching Tilden play for a decade, wrote that his performance against the younger player approached absolute perfection as he overwhelmed Richards 7–5, 6–2, 6–1 in an "awe-inspiring" fifty-nine minutes. It was the way to go.

Pro tournaments never caught on like exhibition tours and were not seen again at the West Side until after the war.

Tilden's career as a professional player went on for another fifteen years. He finally met his master in Ellsworth Vines, after beating Karel Kozeluh, Cochet, Richards, Lott and Lester Stoefen, when Vines won forty-seven out of seventy-three matches on a national tour. He continued to play in exhibitions and to coach, but he had lost most of his inheritance

131

in the Depression and he died a poor and lonely man in 1953 at the age of sixty. His last years were darkened by a prison sentence in California for a homosexual offense, but he refused to be crushed even by that dread experience. In opening his autobiography he wrote:

"For all through my career I have loved the brightness, and I long for it again. . . . My conviction is that the champion of today owes much to the champion of yesterday and even more to the champion of tomorrow."

In the early days of the West Side Stadium the West Side Tennis Club was occasionally visible to the public through reports of its annual meeting and its activities at the USLTA meetings. By the end of the twenties the club had disappeared from view as an organization and in its place there was simply Forest Hills. With its ten-year contract extending to 1934, there were no arguments about what club would hold the big events, and after that the Depression dampened the enthusiasm of West Side's rivals. Then came World War II and it was simply natural, traditional, to hold the championships at Forest Hills.

Even in bad times the club continued to improve its facilities. The present Grandstand next to the Stadium had its origin in temporary stands for 1,500 put up in 1931 and made permanent in 1937 at a cost of $5,000, following criticism of the practice of holding simultaneous matches in the Stadium. At Wimbledon there is only one center court, but there matches can be played until 9:30 in the northern June light. The Garden Café was installed next to the Stadium in 1931, with a bar and umbrella-shaded tables.

As if to enshrine Forest Hills, the USLTA held its Golden Jubilee ceremonies there during the championships in 1931. One hundred and fifty nationals veterans were named to receive medals, and sixty showed up to stand in line in the Stadium while Secretary of the Navy Francis Adams handed them out under the watchful gaze of Julian Myrick, the chairman. Present were Eugenius Outerbridge, Richard Sears, the first great champion, and several of his successors: Slocum, Campbell, Hovey, Whitman, Ward and Wright, as well as contemporary stars like Tilden, Lott and Allison. (Tilden had won three exhibitions two days before at Germantown.) Also there was the first woman champion, Ellen Hansell, and such titlists as Hellwig, Bundy, Homans, Sears, Wightman and Mallory. Tilden got the biggest hand.

Writing for the occasion, A. Wallis Myers of London recalled how in the early days the Wimbledon tourney was adjourned for the Eton–Harrow cricket match at Lord's. "Imagine a two-day halt at Forest Hills in 1931 in order that the fans might migrate to Meadow Brook for polo."

Filing into the marquee, the old-timers passed under words from Kipling's "If":

> . . . if you can meet with triumph and disaster
> And treat those two imposters just the same . . .

15

THE GREAT DEFAULT

HELEN WILLS WAS NOT a colorful personality like Tilden, but then most great tennis players are remembered for their game and not for their life off the court or their extracurricular behavior on it. It was Wills's steady domination of all comers that created her enormous international following and made her newsworthy year after year. Beginning in 1922, she appeared in the finals at Forest Hills nine times. No other player comes close to this record, including Tilden, because for three years the men's championships were held in Philadelphia. Of the nine events, she lost the first in 1922 and the last in 1933.

By 1933 Wills, now Mrs. Moody, had established herself as the greatest woman player in the history of the game. Miss Poker Face made the news wherever she went. She had trained at Berkeley to be an artist and could do accomplished sketches. In Berlin she told reporters that she could do a better sketch of herself than had appeared in the press, and in a few minutes she presented them with one. It was the kind of spontaneous gesture that puzzled reporters, who could not reconcile the friendly, out-going Californian's personal charm with her utterly humorless court behavior.

Off the court she could look the perfect 1920s belle and wear the styles of the times with flair. In later life she designed fashions. When she played tennis she seemed to put on a mask; the famous white sun visor in fact did conceal her features. One suspects that she knew well her own feelings and the need to control them. But the lack of emotional display seemed unnatural, and it was this quality that turned the public briefly against her at the height of her career.

In 1933, after a year's layoff, Moody won at Wimbledon and came to Forest Hills, where she faced Betty Nuthall in the semifinals in a match that offered a moment of minor historical interest. First of all Moody dropped her first set in seven years, losing the opener 2–6. And then, in the second set, she served two games in a row. . . . So much for the alertness of officials. She won the set 6–3 and the third 6–2. But still the rules had been broken. Neither player was aware of the mistake until later, and there was no protest. Moody now had to face the current champion, Helen Jacobs, whom she had beaten in the 1928 finals in straight sets.

The two Helens, paralleling the two Bills, were known as the great rivals among women. Jacobs was not thought to be Moody's equal and was playing as the underdog against a woman who was twenty-eight years old —only two years older than she was.

Helen Jacobs, like Helen Wills Moody, came from California and followed the older girl's traces at the Berkeley Tennis Club, Anna Head School and the University of California. At one point the Jacobs family lived in a house where the Willses had lived. There was, however, acquaintanceship rather than friendship between the two girls.

"We were probably most friendly when I was in the juniors," Jacobs wrote in her autobiography. "In 1924 my mother and I were guests of Mrs. Wightman along with Helen and Mrs. Wills . . . we frequently went shopping together or sat around and chatted." Later, though, "Helen and I were never together off the court for we each had our different personalities and our own friends. Her personality toward opponents was definitely on the cold side. . . ." However, Jacobs insisted there never was a feud as the press claimed.

Jacobs, who had been consistently beaten by Moody since childhood, wanted badly to beat the glacial Queen Helen, and she went to the right person for advice, the one player Moody could not beat, Suzanne Lenglen. Lenglen drilled Jacobs in hitting cross court so that she would avoid giving Moody the backcourt dominance she liked best. For at the net, Jacobs observed, Moody's game was "merely adequate." Jacobs, being faster, was determined to play the net as often as possible.

A crowd of 8,000 came to the Stadium and were stunned by Jacobs' 8–6 victory in the first set. Moody evened it next set, 6–3, but in the third Jacobs broke Moody's serve twice and led 3–0. It looked like a love set was possible, and the end of Queen Helen's reign. This prospect was the more surprising because Jacobs had fainted from fatigue following defeat at Sea Bright by Sarah Palfrey in the final. Moody had changed her tactics in the second set and had won by drop-shotting her opponent, who was exhausted from running. However, Jacobs recovered her strength in the intermission.

Now she stood ready to serve and make it 4–0, for her serve was particularly effective that afternoon. When the ball boy failed to give her balls to start the game, she saw that the receiver had walked over to the umpire and was putting on her sweater.

Allison Danzig says that Jacobs then ran to Moody, and another reporter wrote that she begged Moody to continue, but Jacobs denied this and said she merely inquired if she would like to rest. Moody said no and walked away without shaking hands. Her back, which had been ailing all season, was hurting so much that she felt faint.

Jacobs ran off the court through a portal leading under the Stadium. One can imagine her disappointment in not being able to finish off her obviously sagging opponent. But it had been her own aggressive play that had made Moody stretch and strain until she could no longer stand the pain. Jacobs returned to receive the trophy amid tremendous applause, for she was clearly the better player that day (and no other).

But the feeling was that Moody should have stuck it out and taken her licking. Like Lenglen in 1921, she looked to the press like a quitter. Who can say whether the thought of defeat was more unbearable than physical pain? She told reporters:

"I feel that I have spoiled the finish of the national championships and wish that I had followed the advice of my doctor and returned to California. I still feel I did right in withdrawing because I felt that I was on the verge of a collapse on the court."

It was her first defeat since 1922. Those present as well as viewers of newsreels will never forget the absolutely impassive face and rapid stride as she walked away. Where was the pain? Where was the bad back?

The ill feeling, and the pain too, passed. Two years later at Wimbledon Moody beat Jacobs in three sets and threw her racket in the air for one of the few spontaneous moments of her life on court and put her arm around Jacobs. In 1938 she again beat Jacobs at Wimbledon 6–4, 6–0, after Jacobs sprained her foot.

Then she retired, wrote books, painted and never came back to Forest Hills. Keeping her trophies in a closet, she put tennis out of her life with the same brisk determination she had displayed while making it central to her being for fifteen years. No Tilden she. No Wightman encouraging youngsters and supporting the sport that made her famous. She never saw Helen Jacobs again.

A consequence of the default was that she and Elizabeth Ryan had to default the doubles final. But an exhibition was held in the Stadium, with Alice Marble playing for Moody against Betty Nuthall and Freda James of England. In the second set Nuthall hit an overhead with such force that Marble could not duck in time and took the ball in the eye. The injury was so painful that the champions won by default a second time. It was not one of Forest Hills' best days.

135

Because Moody opposed the wearing of shorts and Jacobs, with stocky legs, wore them, a review of the fashions of Forest Hills may be appropriate at this point. In the phrase of the time, "fashion is spinach." It is also laden with strong feeling, and if "fashion is spinach" can be interpreted to mean that clothes do not make the man or woman, this is a challenge that will always be taken up.

It is fashionable *now* to be unfashionable. The message of the counter-culture is that anything goes, and that ultimately, if the streakers have any point, nothing goes. In the more hierarchical world of the twenties, when the mold of formality began to crack and sports clothes moved from the playing fields to the drawing rooms, tennis costumes remained formal and limited. Bill Tilden could sport his huge cardigan sweaters and pullovers called "grizzlies," and others might wear expensive camel's hair coats in imitation of the polo-playing Hitchcocks and Harrimans, but on the court a rigid formality prevailed. No color was permitted despite the fact that white balls are not very visible against white tennis clothes. The exception was in headdress. Lenglen had her bandeaux, Borotra his beret, Cochet his cap, Wills her eyeshade.

Only the pros have been able to break the white convention in recent years. Right up to the seventies no club permitted anything but whites on the court.

But there was elegance in white flannel trousers, creased and cuffed, going back to the English champion Doherty, and in white ducks, which were adopted as the summer uniform of boys and young men off the court at camp or at resorts. From golf came knickers, but these were inconvenient for tennis, and only one good player, Sidney B. Wood, Jr., ever tried wearing them at Wimbledon—when he was fifteen.

The revolution of the thirties was in the shift to shorts. This had been predicted as early as 1905. Lenglen had introduced the shorter skirt, but even she wore stockings, rolled daringly just above the knee. In 1929 Helen Wills was training with a famous coach, Henri Darsonval, before a small crowd and she wore no stockings. This was a headliner. Pierre Gillou, captain of the French Davis Cup team, issued a statement:

"Mme. Mathieu, our number-one player, wears both stockings and socks. I hope she gets to the finals with Miss Wills."

Wimbledon officials promptly declared stockings *de rigueur,* then backtracked and left the decision to the good taste of the players. Gradually stockings disappeared, but skirts were a fixture until the colorful Lili de Alvarez showed up in 1931 at Wimbledon in shorts—really a split skirt. It was predicted that they would never become popular because they were too unattractive. Later that summer the city of Memphis banned women in shorts from the public courts and ordered men never to remove their tennis shirts.

Then in 1932 the British star Bunny Austin, a Wimbledon finalist and the brother of the girl Alvarez had been playing when she wore shorts, showed up at Forest Hills in shorts. He had not yet worn them at Wimbledon and was using Forest Hills as a test case.

Austin in his memoirs (*A Mixed Double,* 1969) said the idea came to him because of the heat. He thought of rugby and *bought* some shorts in

136

Helen Jacobs, the chief threat to Helen Wills Moody. They were acquainted socially but never close friends, and their rivalry on court was blown up into a feud by the press.

Queen Helen Wills Moody never took to shorts, but just by not wearing long stockings she raised eyebrows. Note the thickness of her right wrist, toughened by practicing a great deal against men.

New York. So shorts were already being worn—but not on the tennis court. At Monte Carlo the hall porter, seeing Austin's bare legs under a polo coat, said, "Excuse me, sir. I think you've forgotten your trousers." He got away with it at Wimbledon in 1933, and even Cochet put on a pair, but only for the mixed doubles. His opponent, Norman Farquharson, rolled up his trousers.

Women immediately adopted the fashion, and when Helen Jacobs appeared in tournaments in shorts, Mrs. Wightman deplored it and forbade shorts at the Wightman Cup matches. But when she beat Moody at Forest Hills in 1933, Jacobs wore white shorts with a black stripe. Next season at Wimbledon Betty Nuthall donned a low-backed dress, and the ultimate in shorts were worn in 1937. Evolution could go no further, at least until Gussie Moran's lace panties were put on display at Wimbledon and Forest Hills in 1949. Pauline Betz managed to upstage Gussie in 1951 by wearing leopard-skin shorts, but that was at Madison Square Garden, not Forest Hills.

Not all the men liked shorts. Borotra, Perry, Crawford, von Cramm never wore them. Don Budge kept the loose-flowing, wide-legged flannels until he turned pro. A psychiatrist suggests that this was a regal symbol, for the monarch always wears more formal garb then his subjects. Today the ruling champion must find some other way to express his or her supremacy. It certainly is not to be found in any of today's costumes.

When Parke Cummings wrote his history of American tennis he predicted that Gussie Moran's lace panties were a passing fad that would never catch on. But some of the women players sport more lace than Gussie would have thought possible, and in doing so, whatever "provocative" quality they once had has been nullified by overdoing it. Perhaps fashion at Forest Hills really is spinach.

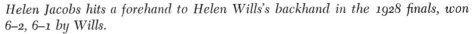

Helen Jacobs hits a forehand to Helen Wills's backhand in the 1928 finals, won 6–2, 6–1 by Wills.

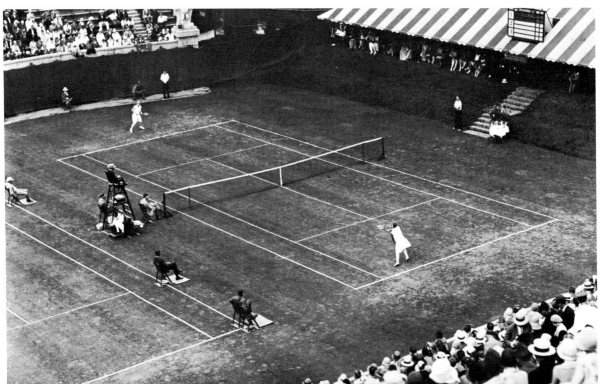

16

THE EARLY THIRTIES

TILDEN'S RETIREMENT DID NOT MEAN the end of great tennis at Forest Hills by any means, but it did mean the end of the game's domination by any single figure. In all the years since, only one man, Fred Perry, has retired the cup by winning three national championships. In later years winners like Kramer and Gonzales turned pro much younger than Tilden did and therefore were not able to play in their prime in the nationals. But the Open has now been played seven times, and only Stan Smith has managed to win it twice; he then failed to reach the finals three successive years.

In the thirties the great players were Vines, Perry and Budge, and some would put Riggs in their class. But the period is remembered for a large number of outstanding players, probably more of them than were around in Tilden's time—players like Allison, Shields, Crawford, Wood, von Cramm, who got to the finals, and others like Mangin, Austin, Sutter, Bell, Grant, Van Ryn, Lott and Stoefen, who had star quality and won a lot of tournaments. If you look at the names of ranking players in the twenties, many are more or less forgotten—King, Holman, Seligson, Hennessey.

Take a ranking of the thirties at random—say, 1934—and you find Allison, Wood, Shields, Parker, Stoefen, Lott, Bell, Sutter, Budge and Grant. Some truly great matches came out of this group of players. In six years of the decade the United States reached the challenge round of the Davis Cup but won it only in 1937 and 1938, against Great Britain and Australia. France continued to hold the cup from 1927 to 1932, and then for four years Great Britain, so dominant in the early days of the cup, beat France, the United States (twice) and Australia. Austin and Perry formed an unbeatable combination.

For a brief while it appeared that Tilden had a successor in Ellsworth Vines, a tall, gangly Californian who often wore a white cap and always hit the ball with tremendous force. But it did not always go in, and his game was uneven. When he was hot, though, he was as spectacular as anyone who has ever played at Forest Hills. And he could be hot and cold in the course of one match.

His chief weapons were a serve faster than any except that of Gonzales and a flat forehand that just skimmed the net with no margin for error. Julius Heldman, a student of tennis style, says that no one ever made more chalk fly than Vines. He was beautiful to watch and immediately won public admiration for his grace, modesty and boyish effortless style of play. His forehand became a pattern for many teachers of tennis and of course was what Kramer modeled his forehand on.

Vines had a curious windmill stroke in which the racket made an almost 360-degree sweep. Starting on high as though he were going to serve, he brought the racket head back almost to the ground and swept up to the ball. Yet he put no spin on it. Imitation of this stroke was fatal for weekend players, and the teachers soon realized it. It made Vines unbeatable in the backcourt and he could return serve with fantastic force.

Junior champion at eighteen, he swept the field the next year at Forest Hills in 1931, knocking off Doeg, the titleholder, Perry, and then Lott in the finals. An ecstatic press predicted a brilliant future for him, and the next season he lived up to expectations. But there were harbingers of coming trouble in one of the great semifinals matches of all time, when he just managed to beat Sutter, the young New Orleans player of consummate style and consistency.

Sutter today preaches percentage tennis—get it back, get it back. Practice, practice, practice. "You can't afford a stroke that is only seventy-five percent effective. It has to work ninety-nine percent of the time," he says. He has two children he trained who are now on Ivy League tennis teams, as proof of his maxim.

His steadiness paid off in the first two sets against Vines that September afternoon in 1932. As Vines made error after error, Sutter kept the ball in, avoiding deep shots as much as possible because he knew Vines was unbeatable at the baseline. He won 6–4, 10–8 and came within a stroke of match point three times in the third set and once in the fourth. But Vines gradually came round, winning the third 12–10, the fourth 10–8, and the last one, when Sutter was tired, 6–1. It took two and a half hours, and the packed Stadium went wild when it ended. Sutter's magnificent challenge was the highlight of the tournament.

The long match had another consequence. It delayed the other semifinal between Cochet and Allison until six o'clock. They played on until they could not see the ball, each taking two sets. The next day Cochet won the match, but was annoyed to have to play the finals the same day against Vines, who won in straight sets before the largest crowd yet. Cochet was tired. Twice he was unable to move out of the way in time to avoid being hit by Vines's blinding serve. The last two aces of the match served by Vines were so hard that they bounced into the stands.

Sailing for home, Cochet told the press that the scheduling of two matches the same day was unfair, no matter how brief the first one was. At Wimbledon this could not happen. He also said something familiar to today's players: "The turf was half wool, half cotton." Meaning a combination of dirt and grass. But he did say that Vines was the better player. Vines had beaten him in the Davis Cup and at New York. Cochet never returned to Forest Hills.

And Vines never reached the finals in 1933. The season was disastrous, and he lost at Forest Hills in the fourth round in straight sets to Bitsy Grant in a triumph of Mutt over Jeff. He turned pro and proved his superiority over the ancient Tilden in a long series of matches across the country, and then over Perry too. He was barely beaten by Budge as a pro and retired from tennis at the age of twenty-eight to play pro golf.

Vines chose to play the game he had, win or lose, and exhaust its possibilities. Once he met his match, he had no desire to be continually humiliated. Like Helen Wills, he had to win or not play at all.

The year that Vines won his second title the West Side Club made some improvements to its facilities. Two new Har-tru clay courts were laid out by H. A. Robinson & Company, the same kind of greenish granular fast-drying surface that will be played on in the 1975 Open. In addition two Bouhana courts were put down by En-Tout-Cas, a French company whose name means "in any event," particularly rain. German red clay from Wiesbaden was put on top of cinders from Washington, D.C., a dumping place for railroad locomotives.

The year 1932 was one of the most gratifying for the West Side.

With Vines gone, the British moved into Forest Hills under the banner of Fred Perry. There was a movie made of Perry in slow motion that showed how fast he was. Missing a shot completely, he was still able to run back and hit it effectively a second time! This speed was his forte, and he combined it with a wristy forehand developed from first playing table tennis, of which he became world champion.

Perry was an enormous crowd pleaser, handsome enough to be a movie star, and a cocky showman in a white blazer and an unlit pipe, as though he were a lord and not the son of a Labor party member of Parliament. He never ruffled anyone with a display of temper, for he was phlegmatic and won his matches by outlasting his opponents. His physical condition was second to none.

After several years of disappointing Davis Cup zone play, Perry finally gave his country its first great champion in fifteen years, and he did it at Forest Hills in 1933. In an exhausting five-set match he defeated the Wimbledon champion from Australia, Jack Crawford. Next June he repeated this triumph at Wimbledon when Crawford foot-faulted at match point on a ball that was otherwise an ace. He was so unnerved that he could not get the second serve over the net.

George Lott considers Perry one of the very great players of all time and points to his record of nine out of ten Davis Cup challenge-round wins, three successive Wimbledon titles, three American titles, a French and an Australian title, all in the four years 1933 to 1936. As a pro, however, he was unable to beat Vines consistently and lost to Budge on an average of three out of four times.

It may be chauvinistic to say this, but one of the most memorable days at Forest Hills was when Perry was beaten in 1935 by the Texan Wilmer Allison. Allison was a famous doubles player until he beat Cochet at Wimbledon in 1930. Ranked number one in 1934 and seeded first, he wound up facing Perry in the 1935 semifinals. So often athletes with handicaps go farther than those with perfect health. An operation in his side forced Allison to hit facing the net. He served this way, not always impressively, since he could not easily stand sideways, but what was a disadvantage in the backcourt made him unequaled at the net, where the correct position is facing forward. Having nothing overwhelming but the volley, he used it devastatingly. With John Van Ryn he swept away all doubles opponents, beginning at Wimbledon in 1929.

His singles game waxed, and in 1934 Allison took Perry to five sets by sheer aggressiveness. He did not like playing at Forest Hills because of

Fred Perry (right) represented the summit of England's achievements in tennis and was a three-time singles titleholder at Forest Hills before turning pro in 1937.

George Lott (middle), volleying here to Ellsworth Vines, was one of the greatest doubles players, a five-time national champion in that category, but he took only one set in this 1931 singles finals.

142

Clifford Sutter (far right) of New Orleans.

the humidity, and played better in Europe or in his native Texas, where the heat was dry. But on this day he conquered his habitual lack of self-confidence and went for the kill, jumping to a 3–1 lead in the first set. Perry pulled even and then, in lunging to return a line drive, he fell on his side heavily. Although he laughed off the shock, his game suffered and later in the match a doctor was brought to the sidelines to keep an eye on Perry, who kept putting his hand to his back.

Just how much of an advantage Allison gained from Perry's injury (it later turned out to be a misplaced kidney) it is not clear. But there was no stopping the American, and he won in straight sets in the best display of tennis of his career. In the finals he easily disposed of Sidney B. Wood, Jr. Having won the singles title, he thereafter confined himself to doubles. With Van Ryn he won the American championship that year, and in 1936 they lost in the final to Budge and C. Gene Mako.

In his last appearance as an amateur at Forest Hills, Perry was charted by the seedings to meet Budge in the finals, and meet they did. Budge was still developing. He had begun in 1934 by winning his first Forest Hills match against Tilden. Next year he was beaten in the quarter-finals by Grant. In 1936 he forced Perry to five sets, winning the first and third sets 6–2, 6–1. Had Perry not turned pro, they probably would have met again at West Side Stadium.

Perry, as most know, eventually went into the tennis-clothes business, his trademark being an embossed laurel wreath. Wearing a blazer and an unlit pipe, he shows up at Forest Hills as a British newspaper correspondent, still lean, handsome and genial. He is remembered as the master of the approach shot and advocate of the continental grip that requires no

change for backhand strokes. His own account of his strokes describes how he studied Cochet's "early-ball game," taking the ball on the rise and giving the opponent less time to get ready, while at the same time moving in as he hit so that the weight of his body provided the pace while his moving feet carried him in toward the net.

The weekend player can learn something from this technique, for so many balls fall short of the baseline that they beg to be moved in on. Perry advises you not to hit such balls hard or you will lose your balance. The momentum of your body will give the ball depth and speed. And if you get good enough you will be able to fool your opponent, as Perry so often did, by disguising where you intend to place the ball.

With Tilden gone, then Vines and then Perry, Forest Hills seemed to be burning up its champions, but in fact it was also producing another very great one, another redhead from California who was to give Forest Hills its ultimate accolade in making it the capstone of the Grand Slam: J. Donald Budge.

This New Yorker *cartoon of the day shows the big hitter Frank Hunter in baggy flannels endangering a linesman.*
DRAWINGS BY JOHAN BULL; © 1929, 1957 THE NEW YORKER MAGAZINE, INC.

The tall drink of water with the dipper is Bill Tilden, keeping his semifinal opponent John Doeg waiting. The ball boy with West Side initials looks a bit old for the job.

144

Bunny Austin, the Englishman who first wore shorts at Forest Hills, in conventional longies.

Perhaps Texan Wilmer Allison's smile is in anticipation of beating Fred Perry.

145

17

THE GRAND SLAM

DON BUDGE WAS THE SON of a Scottish soccer player who moved to California for his health. As a boy he was a natural athlete, and his passion was baseball. Perhaps because he was a right-handed thrower and a left-handed batter, he developed a backhand that has never been equaled. But more than that he developed a flawless game, and with such talent that he was the world's amateur master for two years.

Whatever gifts of bodily movement were in his genes he added to these his own self-discipline, born of a tendency to boyish excess. He may have lost to Perry at Forest Hills in 1936 because he had upset his stomach drinking malteds before the match. It was a curious match. Intermittent rain allowed the players a full hour of rest, yet he found himself exhausted. "My serve in the fifth set was a dishrag," he wrote in his memoirs. Yet he came within two points of upsetting Perry for the title, and barely lost the fifth set, 13–11.

Like Tilden after losing to Johnston, Budge then reformed. He did not need to change any strokes. He had already, under the direction of Tom Stow, the great pro of the Claremont Country Club in Oakland, abandoned the Western for the Eastern grip. He needed to change habits. He wrote later (*Don Budge: A Tennis Memoir*, 1969):

I immediately cut out of my diet all the foods that had turned my stomach sour: chocolates, pastries and other sweets, and fried foods as well . . . I undertook a program of special exercises.

He did sit-ups and deep knee bends and he jogged. In order to avoid the temptation of abandoning jogging because it was so boring, he drove his Packard to the Berkeley Hills, walked up to the ridge and looked at San Francisco Bay as he ran. Eventually he was able to run up to the ridge. His aim was to build fifth-set stamina. In three years he missed only six or seven days working out.

This steadiness of character translated itself not only into wind and strong muscles but also into consistency on the court. From Tilden he learned how essential steadiness is. Big Bill would play him with the proviso that he could have one point per set free from Don whenever he wanted it. As soon as Budge let down, Tilden would grab that extra point. Gradually Budge turned himself into a player who was unbeatable. In 1937 he went to Europe, where he proved to be the new Tilden.

In the interzone Davis Cup he breezed along until he met Baron Gottfried von Cramm, who was playing for Germany at Wimbledon for the right to challenge Great Britain. Budge's five-set victory was in his own view his greatest match. Behind 1–4 in the last set, he attacked von Cramm's service and rushed the net. On the sixth match point Budge won at 8:45 P.M.

Then came the challenge round, and Budge, Parker and Mako brought the Davis Cup back to the United States after four years of British custody. The cup had been abroad for ten years. This deserved something special, and the USLTA arranged for a little parade when the team got off the S.S. *Washington*. They put the team on top of a Fifth Avenue double-decker bus, ran it across 14th Street, up Fifth Avenue and over to the Vanderbilt Hotel. It was pleasing recognition for tennis and helped insure a sellout crowd for the nationals. In fact 5,000 were turned away from the final when Budge again met von Cramm.

Budge admittedly thrived on adulation and was more comfortable at Forest Hills than at Wimbledon with its formalities. Even though von Cramm again carried him five sets, Budge won each of his three by 6–1. With the crowd completely behind him, he never doubted that he would win his first title. And once he had it, he was swamped with offers to turn pro. This was in 1937, when the Depression was still haunting the country. His family was in modest circumstances.

But Don Budge, for all his ebullience and childlike impulse, was a patient man. The pros could wait. The USLTA had made it possible for him to build a tennis career and he believed he owed amateur tennis another season. But he was determined to make it a unique one. He had to do something no one else had yet done.

Having elected to remain amateur, he received the Sullivan Award for the best American athlete of the year, the only tennis player ever to do so.

His plan for the next year was to be the first to win the major championships of the countries which had won the Davis Cup—Australia, France, Great Britain and the United States—and he worked out the way to do it. The secret was to play enough tennis to win but not too much to spoil his game. Crawford had a chance to win the four titles in 1933 but lost at Forest Hills for want of sufficient acclimatizing in the United States.

So Budge spent an extra two weeks in Australia before he entered the test matches, which he refused to tense up about. He won everything in Australia without losing a set. In France he dropped one set and at Wimbledon he won again without losing a single set in the tournament; he beat Austin after having watched an older woman put top spin on her backhand. Even at the height of his game Budge was always prepared to correct a fault, and like Tilden he had been undercutting his best stroke in a defensive instead of offensive way. He then won the doubles with Mako and mixed doubles with Alice Marble, something only Riggs and Sedgman have been able to do after winning the singles title.

When he went after the national title at Forest Hills in 1938, there was no such thing as the Grand Slam. It was simply a gleam in Budge's eye. His confidence was high after he had helped hold the Davis Cup against Australia's challenge at Germantown, but his health was poor. He kept losing his voice. A doctor prescribed removal of an offending tooth. He came to the tournament in marvelous shape and beat Van Horn, Kamrath, Nare, Hopman and Wood to reach the finals. To some it looked like a setup for Budge, but as Budge remarked, "Gene Mako was as likely to roll over and play dead for me as peace was to come in our time." This was the month Chamberlain went to Munich to settle matters with Hitler. In fact Mako took the second set and that was the second set that Budge lost in four tournaments.

Budge does not like the fact that some people thought he threw a set to his pal. His argument against this dishonorable idea is built around the quality of Forest Hills tennis:

> In the finals of a tournament of the stature of Forest Hills, I cannot imagine anyone taking the chance of willingly losing a set. . . . [Furthermore] this was *this* Forest Hills, the fourth to my Grand Slam set, and under those special circumstances I would not even have *mused* on the possibility of giving up a single point to anyone, even if I were ahead 6–0, 6–0, 5–0, 40–love. . . . When at last I hit the shot that won Forest Hills and the Grand Slam, when I rushed to the net, the man who was there to take my hand and congratulate me and smile at my triumph, was the only other man in the world who knew what I had really accomplished and how much I cared.

148

When the press reported on Budge's triumph there was no reference to the Grand Slam. The term was later used by Budge himself, copying Bobby Jones's Grand Slam in golf—winning the U.S. and British amateur and open championships in one season. The idea stuck and the Grand Slam did not recur until Maureen Connolly managed it in 1953 and Rod Laver in 1962. Jimmy Connors *claimed* the Grand Slam in 1974 after beating Rosewall at Forest Hills, but he had been barred from the French championships and could not have meant this literally.

Whoever goes after the Grand Slam should remember what it takes—really wanting those four trophies and not caring too much about anything else that year. It is not an easy task for a pro who is committed to keep playing week in, week out all over the world.

Which is just one more reason that many people feel that Don Budge was the greatest of all. To him today this is academic. Like Tilden and many other great players, he has stayed with the game as a teacher and social player, and he still loves to take the court at Forest Hills during the Open. He is a bit heavier than when he beat Mako, and he no longer wears long trousers.

Budge's female counterpart was Californian Alice Marble, a worthy successor to Helen Wills and a woman who played much like a man. Her serve was as powerful as those of many men. Here we have one more player from an athletic family—one brother a handball champ, another a minor league baseball prospect—who started out playing baseball (Budge and Talbert likewise), suffered bad health (tuberculosis), slumped in her game and worked to overcome her faults with the famous Eleanor "Teach" Tennant. She won the finals four times at Forest Hills as well as four doubles titles (with Sarah Palfrey) and four mixed doubles (with Mako, Budge, Hopman and Riggs).

In 1936 Alice defeated "Little Helen" Jacobs, ending Jacobs's four-year reign, after dropping the first set. Her strongest shot was the volley. After a bad season in 1937, when the Chilean Anita Lizana became the first foreign titleholder in our women's singles, Marble came back to take the next three titles and won at Wimbledon in 1939. She was pretty, wore shorts well, and her personality was attractive. For a time she sang in nightclubs.

After winning Wimbledon, she had to work to beat Jacobs in three sets at Forest Hills. The adversary of both players was a wind of gale force. Jacobs's weaker strokes put her at a disadvantage against the wind, and she dropped the first set 6–0, only to find her way in the second and escape from match point five times before losing in the third. Marble was voted the outstanding woman athlete of the year by the sportswriters, who honored her a second time in the same fashion in 1940, when she beat Margaret Osborne in straight sets and then turned pro to tour with Budge, Tilden and Mary Hardwick, the English star.

Marble was one of the great women doubles players, and in Sarah Palfrey (now Mrs. Jerry Danzig) she had the perfect partner. Allison Danzig (no relation) called Sarah "America's sweetheart of tennis." She came from New England and played with a steadiness and stubbornness

Sept. 7, 1935   THE   Price 15 cents

THE NEW YORKER

that carried her to two singles titles in 1941 and 1945, the last against Helen Jacobs, who had beaten her for the championship in 1934 and 1935. With Nuthall she won the doubles in 1930 and 1933, with Jacobs in 1934 and 1935, and with Marble she held the title for five years, from 1937 to 1941. Altogether in doubles and singles she appeared in thirteen finals at West Side Stadium. A member of the West Side, she still plays there regularly.

In *Winning Tennis and How to Play It* (1946) she tells of her embarrassment in 1930 when her bra strap broke during the finals of the doubles. Here was where that safety pin in the umpires' "veranda" would have come in handy, but Sarah's sister produced the needed pin from her purse.

To say that the thirties ended with Bobby Riggs is certainly not to say that they died with a whimper. His matches with Margaret Court and Billie Jean King may deceive a young public into considering him a clown and nothing more than a self-promoter. He was in his day just about the brainiest player in big-time tennis. On the court or off, Bobby has always been figuring the angles. He is an American Tom Jones, a picaresque character living by his wits.

Ed Baker, former executive secretary of the USLTA, recalls the first time he met Riggs. It was in the USLTA office in New York and Riggs wanted to use the phone—long distance. He was told he would have to pay for toll calls. Bobby had no money beyond what he could pick up playing "amateur" tennis.

"Tell you what I'll do," said the cocky little bantam. "I'll flip you for it."

Riggs's gambling is hardly destructive. He won over $100,000 from English bookies when he bet he would win the singles, doubles and mixed doubles in one year at Wimbledon in 1939. Then he came to Forest Hills with the reputation of being the bad boy of tennis.

"I think of myself as someone who was programmed to become an athlete of some kind," he wrote in *Court Hustler* (1973). The program was his own and did not suit amateur authorities, who tried to keep him in California as a junior. His aggressiveness found him ready sponsors, and he boasts of being on the payroll of C. Lynch, of the brokerage house Merrill Lynch, for $200 a week while playing as an amateur. A local club

Without casting any aspersions on the player who turns pro, this 1935 New Yorker cover explains Tilden's changing psychology, which was far ahead of that of the amateur associations that ran the tournaments.

By the late thirties West Side Stadium's vines gave it a venerable air. Crowds queued patiently for tickets. Cars still had running boards. The Japanese flag came down a few years later.

152

Don Budge, the most impressive player after Tilden, invented the Grand Slam by winning the nationals in Australia, France, England and the United States.

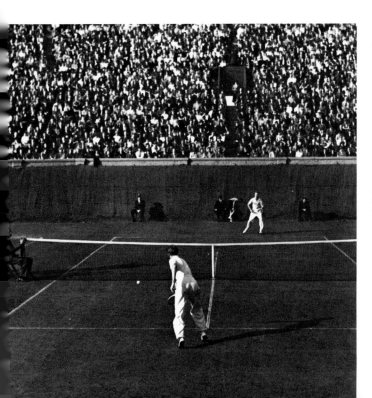

Prancing Sarah Palfrey (far left) won the title in 1941 and 1945. And, just for fun, in 1974 she was a winner of a round robin at the West Side for the press.

Alice Marble (middle), a four-time titlist in the thirties.

Budge, in the near court (left), packs 'em in at the 1938 finals, in which he beat Gene Mako.

153

Sept. 10, 1938 THE NEW YORKER Price 15 cents

in Neenah, Wisconsin, handed him $500 for playing there. None of this kept him off the Davis Cup. He was all the U.S.A. had after Budge turned pro.

In the 1939 nationals, which started four days after World War II broke out, Riggs beat unranked Welby Van Horn in the finals in straight sets. Next year, though, Forest Hills cost him money. In a slump he lost his title to W. Donald McNeill before a small crowd of 6,000 and had to abandon his plans for turning pro for a year. In 1941 he returned to West Side Stadium and, after dropping the first set to the clowning Frank Kovacs, finished him in straight sets with little trouble.

As a pro, Riggs had trouble at first beating Budge, but by 1946 Don had slowed down—he even wore glasses—and Riggs took the pro title at Forest Hills and all of $1,200. As he proved against Margaret Court as a middle-aged man, Riggs could out-think, if not out-play, most opponents. In one match between Riggs and Van Horn, Van Horn imprudently said between the third and fourth set that Riggs looked tired, which Riggs was faking. Indignantly Bobby said, "I'm okay. Let's skip the break." Van Horn foolishly went along and was soon exhausted and lost.

But subterfuge could take the form of tricky dink shots and placements that startled players who seemingly had more power and style. Talbert calls Riggs the most underrated of the major players. He was overshadowed by Budge, but he gave Forest Hills customers the kind of gutsy playing they have come to look for.

As the thirties ended, ivy-covered Forest Hills looked more and more like an old institution, but it was only twenty-five years since the first of the nationals had been played there. Yet it was set in its ways. It was not until 1939 that an electric clock was installed, and much was made of buying a gasoline-driven roller for the courts. The cost of tickets had more than doubled, to $1.10 a day, and scalpers had set up shop in houses adjacent to the club grounds.

In 1940 the media began to organize, and newsmen played a tournament of their own, won by Bob Considine. During the war John Kieran of *The New York Times* joined Boris Karloff in the Stadium in an exhibition to raise money for British relief.

And 1940 was also the year that Forest Hills programs carried a Du Pont ad announcing nylon racket strings.

A New Yorker cover in 1938 pokes *fun at the unexplainable habit of carting several rackets on court before a match. Notice the reporters.*

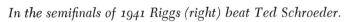

Eschewing the clowning that would come in the seventies, Bobby Riggs won the nationals in 1938 and 1941.

In the semifinals of 1941 Riggs (right) beat Ted Schroeder.

PART III

MODERN TIMES: 1942-1975

18

THE BIG GAME

TENNIS WAS LESS AFFECTED by World War II than by World War I. The forties represent a continuum featuring excellent players: Schroeder, Hunt, Talbert, Mulloy, Sabin, Prusoff, Segura and Falkenburg among the men; and Betz, Brough, Jedrzejowska and Osborne among the women. International competition, of course, ceased, and this took something away from the quality of play and set back European and Australian development several years. The forties were American years, and when the Davis Cup challenge round came to the West Side in 1947 for the first time in a quarter of a century, the crowds saw Americans win three successive years against Australia.

Schroeder played throughout the decade and ranked second from 1946 to 1948. He was a formidable doubles partner to Kramer, and the two held the national doubles title in 1940, 1941 and 1947. Teaming with Parker in 1948, Schroeder got to the finals at Longwood, but they could not beat the great Mulloy–Talbert combination.

Joe Hunt beat Kramer in four sets at Forest Hills in 1943 and might have challenged him continually had he not died as a Navy pilot in an accident off Daytona Beach in 1945.

The singles titles in 1944 and 1945 were won by that indefatigable perennial Frank Parker, a quiet, handsome and persistent player who was in the first ten from 1933 to 1949. In both finals he beat Talbert, who was four times national doubles champion with Mulloy and later a very popular Davis Cup captain.

Parker was a Midwesterner developed on public courts and later coached by the great Mercer Beasley. His defense was stubborn and he made few errors. It is interesting to watch him still, a deliberate, unsmiling senior player eschewing speed and getting the ball back consistently without having overpowering shots.

He was good enough in 1947 to take the first two sets from Kramer in the finals in West Side Stadium. His playing that day won the crowd, and it was reported that the ovation he received was not only greater than Kramer's but greater than any ever heard before in the Stadium.

Bill Talbert was one of the best doubles players the game has known. Forest Hills did not see him and Mulloy win the title in 1942, 1945, 1946 and 1948 because the championships were played at Longwood, but in the 1948 5–0 win over Australia's Davis Cup team they gratified the West Side crowd with a four-set victory over Sidwell and Long. The next year they lost there to Sidwell and Bromwich.

Talbert, a diabetic, has made tennis his life's great avocation. He never turned pro, but took the sensible view toward the patronage of amateur tennis that it could not make you rich. "What the game does offer," he wrote in his memoir, *Playing for Life* (1958), "is something that probably beats money: a chance to live well without it."

Parenthetically, let us remember that this applied only to the very best players on the amateur circuit. At Sea Bright average players without social or athletic cachet were put up at the unfashionable Peninsula Hotel and sent home as soon as they lost their matches. Forest Hills did not even feed the players a free sandwich. The Nassau Country Club fed players in a separate dining room. As Allison Danzig has said, "Amateur players were peasants, just peasants."

Talbert's devotion to tennis has made him as fine a theorist as the game has produced. His three books on stroke making, written with physicist Bruce Old, a college roommate of Bitsy Grant's, represent the ultimate in combining championship experience with scientific study of the game and should be in the library of any player who helps his game by reading the masters. At the 1975 Open, Bill Talbert will be seen from time to time before the microphone in front of the marquee at West Side Stadium.

The name of Jack Kramer—Jake, as he was called as a player—is so well known today that it hardly seems thirty years since he burned up the turf at Forest Hills. He represents a double transition in tennis—to the "big game" of serve and volley, and to the big money of world professionalism.

As a boy he played with Vines and from him learned to hit with power. Defense was not his style. His personality was radically different

Left: Ball boys have other duties.

Below: Every day the draw sheet must be flown to the printer so that the programs will be accurate for the following day's matches.

Top: An electronic scoreboard, courtesy of a tobacco company,
is located above the Stadium marquee.

Bottom left: On to do battle.

Bottom right: If insignia indicate passion, this lady is in love.

Opposite: It's not deep depression—simply official concentration.

Left: A ball girl races Ken Rosewall to "clear the ball."

Below: The umpire checks the net height with a yardstick as two models show off current tennis wear.

Opposite: Connors power.

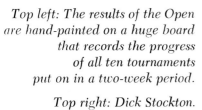

Top left: The results of the Open are hand-painted on a huge board that records the progress of all ten tournaments put on in a two-week period.

Top right: Dick Stockton.

Right: Ilie Nastase.

*Many of the great players stayed at the Forest Hills Inn
in the old days.*

*A picturesque closed bridge links the elevated station platform
directly with the old Forest Hills Inn—now an apartment house.*

Right: Station Square,
seen from the Long Island Railroad
platform.
The West Side clubhouse
is one block to the right.

Below: The garden of a home
a block from the inn.
Today the houses
in this private enclave
sell for $100,000 to $400,000.

from Vines's, though. He was not a gambler who risked all to make the chalk fly. Kramer was calculating in more than one sense. He figured thus: tennis is too fast a game to allow a player the luxury of making decisions once the ball is in play. Not only should rallies be reduced to a minimum in order to reduce the chances of error, but certain shots should be played the same way every time. *"I always hit every short forehand down the line,"* he wrote in his article in *The Fireside Book of Tennis* (1972),

> unless, of course, I have an easy high ball that I can put away crosscourt with no chance of error. Then, when I come in, my opponent will either hit the backhand down the line where I am waiting or he will try one of the most difficult shots in the game, the short backhand crosscourt, which only Don Budge and Frank Kovacs could ever hit consistently. Most opponents will flail at the ball, making 20% placements to 80% errors, so that the percentage is with me.

This is not very romantic or even very colorful, and Tilden was appalled by the implications of the big game, which indeed still has its detractors among spectators who want long rallies. With the rise of European clay-court stars like Borg, long rallies are coming back and there is bound to be a reaction to the boring character of looping backcourt exchanges that exhaust player and spectator alike.

"There is nothing that Jack Kramer does today that players of the past have not done equally well," Tilden wrote in 1950 (*How to Play Better Tennis,* Cornerstone Library). He maintained that the imitation of Kramer produced a generation of young players who lacked adequate training in the fundamentals. The USLTA, he felt, was to blame for promoting the serve-volley style among juniors. For what it is worth, from 1956 to 1968 no American won the national title at Forest Hills. However, the Australians, who dominated tennis after Kramer and Gonzales turned pro, were big-game players themselves.

Once a technique in any sport proves effective, there is no turning back. Just as the Arlberg technique gave way to the parallel in skiing, championship tennis has departed from the "strokier" style because Kramer proved that a fast serve puts so much pressure on the receiver that, except on the slowest surface, a speedy race to the net brings the server in position to win frequently on the next shot. The requirement is a first serve that goes in most of the time, and Kramer developed it.

Analysts since Kramer's day have taken to scientific study of matches to prove what has long been obvious, that the serve is the most important stroke in tennis. Talbert and Old note in their book *Stroke Production in the Game of Tennis* that the server can win outright by ace or error 18 to 30 percent of the time, that the server can lose on the return of serve 12 to 15 percent of the time. Between 40 and 60 percent of all serves are returned and then the players have an equal chance of winning.

One other point about Kramer's game worth noting is that he kept

Don McNeill of Oklahoma beat Riggs for the title in five sets in 1940 after winning a heatedly disputed call.

Dressed in outfits of the Gay Nineties, players put on an exhibition match in 1942 to celebrate the West Side's fiftieth anniversary.

Handsome Frank Parker never gave up until he had won two titles, in 1944 and 1945. His gameness in losing to Jack Kramer in 1947 drew the greatest ovation ever heard at West Side Stadium.

working his way to the net at all times. Instead of planting himself for his ground strokes and taking them sideways, he came at them from behind on the run and hit them in a more open stance. After he hit the ball, his stride carried him to the service line for the volley. As Perry observed, an advantage of the running ground stroke is that it is easy on the arm because it requires less arm power, the weight of the body giving pace to the stroke. But it calls for legs of steel.

Kramer trained rigorously yet suffered physical setbacks more than once. Appendicitis kept him out of the nationals in 1942 and the next year he got ptomaine poisoning and lacked the stamina to beat Joe Hunt. At Wimbledon in 1946 hand blisters made it easier for Drobny, the Czech star, to beat him. But that season he beat Tom Brown in straight sets in a Forest Hills finals that was rated a toss-up, and he repeated the victory in the same fashion in the famous match against Parker the following year, after humiliating Brown at Wimbledon 6–1, 6–3, 6–2.

Turning pro, Kramer put Riggs to flight at Forest Hills next June before 9,000, and Riggs became Kramer's boss for a while as promoter. Riggs signed Gonzales to provide competition for Kramer, but neither he nor Segura got close to beating Kramer consistently. So with no more worlds to conquer except that of Riggs's promotional world, Kramer became a promoter. His innovation was to bring bigness into money making as he had into the game itself. By expanding the game beyond the U.S.A. to the world at large, Kramer injected a new internationalism into the pro game and laid the groundwork for open tournaments. Air travel, of course, made this development possible, and after 1958 jets allowed players to play more frequently in different parts of the world.

In the fifties Forest Hills became a major marketplace where the amateurs were sized up and, if they were good enough, signed up for Kramer's world tours. Of these marathon one-night stands Kramer tired eventually and he settled in California to run a country club and many other lucrative enterprises. Kramer's knowledge of tennis was valuable in educating a new generation of TV spectators as a commentator at Forest Hills matches and elsewhere. He is now in charge of the powerful Association of Tennis Professionals, under attack as a monopoly union of players.

His successor at Forest Hills in 1948 and 1949 was the sullen Mexican-American, Richard "Pancho" Gonzales. Gonzales brought nothing new to the game in the way of strokes, but he had probably as much power as any player in history, and he had a temperament General Patton would have admired. He was constantly sore at someone. Today he calls the quintessential winning quality "the killer instinct."

There is reason to suspect that there is a degree of affectation in his hotheadedness. He possesses a passion very much under his control and he uses it shrewdly. Like Tilden, he dreamed of a career as an entertainer (his father, a Mexican immigrant, worked as a painter in Hollywood movie studios). But chance carried Pancho into public-court tennis. He was big, powerful and so enamored of the game that he skipped school; this

Bill Talbert, who got to the finals in 1944 and 1945, held the doubles title four times and was Davis Cup captain for five years.

Guess who? Bill Talbert as a junior. (He is not putting two hands on the racket.)

165

Francisco Segura brought his two-handed backhand to Forest Hills in 1942, reached the semifinals but failed to go farther until he turned pro in 1947.

The Big Game is associated with Jack Kramer, the finest player after Budge's reign.

Pancho Gonzales won the singles at Forest Hills in 1948 and 1949, and the senior masters in 1974.

For eight years in a row, 1942 to 1950, Margaret Osborne du Pont (left) and Louise Brough (right) held the U.S. doubles title. Louise won the singles from Margaret in 1947; Margaret took the title away next year and held it twice again.

enraged Perry Jones, the California tennis czar, who suspended him from tournament play.

His first appearance at Forest Hills in 1947 at the age of nineteen was *pro forma* for a boy with only one season on grass courts. Next year on the Eastern circuit his performance was mediocre and earned him a bottom seeding at the nationals. Then suddenly Arthur Larsen went down to him in five sets and Parker faced him in the quarterfinals. In four sets the lad with the scar on his dark cheek (not from a knife but a car accident) beat the favored player. The semis brought up Drobny, who also managed to win only a set from Gonzales.

The finals against Eric Sturgess, the South African champion, were scheduled after the women's finals between Margaret Osborne du Pont and Louise Brough. Unfortunately for the men the third set, won by Mrs. du Pont, set a record for length in women's finals, 15–13, and the sun was already going down when play began. After dropping two sets, Sturgess pressed to win the third and force a postponement of the rest of the match to the next day. The weather was foul and the court was slippery.

The score went to 12–12. When you consider the drama of long sets like that, tie breakers seem artificial. (However, that year's mixed doubles of Talbert–du Pont over Falkenburg–Moran, going 27–25, was perhaps a bit ridiculous.) Gonzales feared that a postponement might bring forth a new Sturgess, and he dug in to win 14–12 in near darkness. Perhaps the fading light aided the winner's serve, which was clocked once at 118 miles an hour.

Gonzales did not consider Sturgess as strong a challenge as Schroeder presented the next year. Schroeder had won the title in 1942 and did not appear at Forest Hills in singles except in Davis Cup challenge rounds, in which he won consistently. In 1949 he and Gonzales were Davis Cup teammates and they beat Australia 4–1 (Talbert and Mulloy dropped the doubles to Sidwell and Bromwich).

Schroeder, now twenty-eight, was seeded first. He was no Kramer, but neither was Gonzales at this point. Gonzales is associated with long sets—recall the record 22–24 first set against Charlie Pasarell at Wimbledon in 1969—and the first set went to Schroeder 18–16, the longest since Doeg's 16–14 win over Shields in 1930. To come back and win after such a heartbreaker requires more than anger, and there was reason for anger because the next to last point looked like a bad call in Schroeder's favor.

Pancho dropped the second set 6–2, but in the third he poured it on and won four straight games without letting one go to deuce. With this momentum he closed out the three sets with championship play. He double-faulted only once. On the last point the call against Schroeder brought a cry of dismay from him and he swung his racket as if to throw it at the umpire. But then he smiled and congratulated the plucky Pancho. It was one of the greatest matches of all time.

Gonzales immediately went pro and engaged in a turbulent playing career marked by bitter disputes with Kramer about money. At first he

Joe Hunt might have been one of the greats had he not been killed in a Navy plane accident in 1945. In 1943 he beat Kramer for the title.

could not win and for a while he strung rackets. Eventually he became the greatest box office draw of all, and there are those who rate him above all players. Still dour, he is a teaching pro now and the old lion of Forest Hills, who sparkled in the 1974 Grand Masters tournament, an easy winner at forty-six, his hair long and beginning to gray.

Vijay Amritraj got some coaching from Pancho that year and told the press: "Pancho says I don't have the killer instinct; I say I do." But he said it with a smile. Maybe Pancho meant: if you want to win, scowl.

Southern California's Darlene Hard and Australia's Neale Fraser, both of whom won singles titles at Forest Hills in 1960. Darlene beat Maria Bueno for the title and repeated the victory the next year against Ann Haydon of Great Britain.

19

LITTLE MO AND ALTHEA

THERE WERE ONLY 2,500 in West Side Stadium in 1951 when sixteen-year-old Maureen Connolly beat Doris Hart in three tense sets for her first title. She was the second youngest national champion in history, the youngest having been May Sutton, the 1904 champion. On the last point she let out a scream and threw her racket in the air, and after she left the court she began weeping. Her coach, Eleanor "Teach" Tennant, almost fainted from anxiety as the match ended.

"Little Mo," a New York *Post* writer christened her, recalling the battleship *Missouri*, the Big Mo, on which General MacArthur accepted the Japanese surrender. She had something of MacArthur's victory-mindedness; playing with unsmiling steadiness and dreadnought power, this stubby Californian was quickly acknowledged the best woman player since Helen Wills. It was no trouble almost filling the Stadium the following year to see a rematch with Hart.

For all her youth and diminutiveness Maureen Connolly did not win everyone's heart. She could smile off the court, but she could also be brusque with the press. Perhaps the press sometimes deserves this treatment when it moves in on a player right after a match and lays down a barrage of questions while he is still catching his breath.

But she was a joy to watch. A winner can do no wrong. "My ambition is to play perfect tennis. Then I will always win," she said in England, where she won Wimbledon over Brough in straight sets in 1952. Her court temperament was cool and exemplary. It was her youth that set her apart. So great so young—what a career lay ahead!

In 1953 she went to Australia and won the championship, then to Paris and won the French title too. At Wimbledon she met Doris Hart again, who threw every conceivable shot at her to no avail. Little Mo came to Forest Hills that year seeking the first Grand Slam since Budge had done it when she was only four.

There were 12,000 in the Stadium, and Doris Hart was in her fifth finals. But she could not beat Maureen and in fact did not do as well as she had at Wimbledon. In forty-nine minutes the eighteen-year-old girl from San Diego swept Doris away 6–2, 6–4, and the Grand Slam was hers! Ahead lay the possibility of holding the title a decade or longer.

But an accident ended her career shortly after she won at Wimbledon in 1954. She was a skilled horseback rider, but on this fatal day, riding a horse given to her by a group of San Diegans, she was thrown after the animal had been frightened by a passing cement truck, which it brushed against, crushing her right leg. She recovered well enough to walk but not to play tennis. Norman Brinker married her and the famous Wimbledon stylist Teddy Tinling made her wedding gown. At the age of thirty-four, when Margaret Court was being hailed as Little Mo's equal, as the player who might have displaced her at the top, Maureen Connolly died of cancer.

The sadness of this story lies in part in the public's yearning for a champion to reign for a long time. It seldom happens. After Maureen came a succession of brilliant players: Hart (who won the title in 1954 and 1955), Fry, Gibson, Hard, and then the twin greats, Margaret Smith Court and Billie Jean Moffitt King. None of them accomplished her record of winning thirteen major titles and losing only one match in a scant three years.

Althea Gibson was not as strong a player as Maureen, but her appearance at Forest Hills was a sensation because she was the first black player in the national championships. Since 1917 blacks had their own segregated organization, ironically named the American Tennis Association. This Jim Crow arrangement was accepted as the nature of things. The ATA was a middle-class organization that was not out to rock any boats.

But Althea was not middle-class. She came from a sharecropper family that had moved to Harlem. At one point Althea was on welfare. This was before the days of militancy, before the Supreme Court ordered desegregation of schools. When she won the ATA girls' national championship in 1944 and 1945, she did not think of Forest Hills; she thought of the women's ATA title, which she subsequently earned ten times.

Until after World War II it was out of the question for a black to break into USLTA tournaments. In 1929 the National Association for the Ad-

Maureen Connolly (far court) was one of the all-time great women players, in a class with Wills, Court and King. Here Little Mo drops the ball at Doris Hart's feet in the 1952 finals.

vancement of Colored People—not the ATA!—publicly protested the exclusion of blacks from the junior nationals at the exclusive Seventh Regiment Armory in New York. The executive secretary of the USLTA, Edward B. Moss, said blandly that players must belong to a club. "In pursuing this policy," he added, "we make no reflection upon the colored race, but we believe that as a practical matter, the present method of separate associations for the administration of the affairs and championships of colored and white players should be continued."

And it was continued until 1948, when Reginald Weir, a forty-year-old black physician, was allowed to play in the national indoors at the Seventh

The American Wightman Cup team of 1949 posed on the lawn in front of the West Side clubhouse. Seated are Gertrude "Gussie" Moran, Patricia Todd, Beverly Baker and Shirley Fry. Standing are (left to right) Doris Hart, Louise Brough, Margaret Osborne du Pont and Mrs. Richard Buck, nonplaying captain. They played at Haverford, Pennsylvania, and beat Great Britain 7–0.

Regiment itself. This did not immediately open Forest Hills to Althea, but she played the national indoors in 1949 and 1950 and finally got into the Eastern Grass Court Championships at Orange after Alice Marble in her monthly column in *American Lawn Tennis* spoke out in the interest of fair play.

That championship tennis was a lily-white sport was reprehensible, and the blame for this generally falls on the clubs and the tony people who ran the USLTA. But baseball could not be said to be a genteel, suburban pastime, and when Jackie Robinson joined the Brooklyn Dodgers in 1947 there was a negative reaction among the players. Segregation was a national disease. The West Side Club was no more to blame than the hotel in Portland, Oregon, that once made the great singer Marian Anderson ride to her room in the freight elevator. No tennis player ever objected to competing with Althea Gibson.

Gussie Moran's lace panties were a postwar sensation. The dazzling Californian played well enough to join the pros.

When she got her chance at Forest Hills in 1950, the luck of the draw pitted her against the Wimbledon champion, Louise Brough, in the Stadium in the second round. The champion stepped off to a 6–1 first set against the nervous Harlem woman. Althea looked like she would lose quickly, and there were those who did not conceal their hope that she would be beaten and that would be the end of such people at Forest Hills.

But the thin-legged black girl came back to take the second set. People on the clubhouse veranda watching Ginger Rogers play drifted over to the Stadium to see what Louise could do now. The answer was not very much. Althea came on strong and was leading 7–6. For some time it had been thundering. Suddenly the clouds broke and it came down by the bucketful, and lightning flashed right overhead. The thunderclap was deafening, and something crashed to the ground behind the Stadium—one of the concrete eagles on the parapet had been hit.

The combination of the storm, the interruption and the symbolic eagle falling did nothing for Althea's nerves. The next day she made the mistake of reading the morning papers and she came to the West Side with a sense of doom. Her premonition was justified, and Louise finished her off in eleven minutes in front of five movie cameras and fifteen photographers.

Six years passed before Althea got to a finals at Forest Hills, at the age of twenty-nine, losing to Shirley Fry 6–3, 6–4. But 1957 was her year. She went to Wimbledon and beat Darlene Hard decisively. That rated a parade up Broadway and a lunch at the Waldorf in honor of New York's native daughter. When she got to the Forest Hills finals against Brough, she was ready and Louise was not. Score 6–3, 6–2, and America had its first black tennis champion of either sex. She received the trophy from the Vice-President of the United States, Richard Nixon.

Reaching the heights late, Althea had one good year left and took the title a second time in 1958, beating Darlene Hard in three sets. The year after that the aggressive little Maria Bueno of Brazil rose to the top. Althea, now a pro, shows up for veterans' matches at Forest Hills. She works in the Pepsi-Cola program, developing young players.

An unusual ground-level shot of Louise Brough serving against Doris Hart. Hart held the title in 1954 and 1955.

177

Althea Gibson, the girl from Harlem, broke racial barriers to win the women's title in 1957 and 1958.

It is remarkable that Althea got as far as she did. New York has over 500 public courts, but they are hardly sufficient for a city of 7 million. The year Althea won her second title, there was public criticism of the inadequate support of tennis in New York. The best tennis in Harlem was at the Cosmopolitan Club, to which Althea had been given a membership. For a black to join a white club was still not done.

But Ralph Bunche, then assistant secretary of the United Nations, sought with his son to join the West Side in 1959, and the roof fell in on the club president, Wilfred Burglund, who Bunche said had told him that Negroes and Jews were not accepted for membership. The incident was front-page news, and five days later Burglund resigned as president and Bunche was invited to join the club. Today Arthur Ashe is an honorary club member, and during the Open there are black pros, umpires and spectators on the veranda.

Yet where are the black *players?* Well, on the West Side's clay courts during the 1974 Open there were black kids playing off the finals of the National Junior Tennis League, which engages 100,000 youngsters in competition in forty-five cities, the majority of them minority members. Pepsi-Cola is sponsoring an inner-city tennis development program that may pay off in increasing awareness of the possibilities of tennis as a sport. But no one expects to see the kind of participation that occurs among blacks in track, boxing and the traditional ball sports.

Racial prejudice has never prevented anyone from *playing* tennis. But it is not a sport for the poor, as has been already noted. Because it has been associated with substantial people, the game has drawn hostility from ghetto kids, who, in an understandable reaction, call it a "sissy" sport. The USLTA, belatedly perhaps but commendably, has set up a National Tennis Development Program that will reach the underprivileged.

20

DOWN UNDER ON TOP

THE ARRIVAL OF FRANK SEDGMAN was the handwriting on the wall for West Side Stadium. His victories in 1951 and 1952 foretold the coming preeminence of his fellow countrymen from Australia. Until Sedgman no one from down under had ever won the American title. After Seixas and Trabert almost no one *but* Australians won it, until Arthur Ashe rescued the national honor in 1968.

To be eclipsed nationally in championship tennis for over a decade was more devastating at the time than it is in the perspective of the broader internationalizing of the game under professional sponsorship. The crowd in Ramona, California, on May 13, 1973, was hoping an Australian, Margaret Court, would beat Bobby Riggs. India's Vijay Amritraj and Sweden's Björn Borg were more popular at the 1974 Open than America's Jimmy Connors or Roscoe Tanner.

The decline of American tennis in the fifties and sixties may well have helped to establish the primacy of the Open concept over the outdated amateur fantasy. The failure of a single American to reach the finals at Forest Hills between 1953 and 1963 somewhat soured the public taste for the nationals. The constant disappearance into professional ranks of foreign stars to whom spectators gave their allegiance led to increasing dissatisfaction with the way big-time tennis was being run. But at the same time it helped the fans adjust to seeing non-Americans in the game. It was a period of transition.

Two Americans stood out, Trabert and Seixas, but neither name has the same connotation of a Kramer or a Laver. Trabert took the title in 1953 and 1955, and Seixas took it the intervening year, 1954. Trabert indeed was America's hope after Gonzales, but he quickly turned pro. A protégé of Bill Talbert, he beat Seixas for the championship in fifty-nine minutes in 1953 and distinguished himself in the 3–2 victory over Australia to bring the Davis Cup home for a year. In a sort of revenge the Australian Hartwig eliminated Trabert at Forest Hills next year in the quarterfinals. Seixas, who had been on that winning Davis Cup team, then leveled Hartwig to take the title.

Hartwig did not reach the quarters in 1955, and Seixas was eliminated by Rosewall in the semis. Trabert's straight-set defeat of Lew Hoad put him on the pinnacle and into the hands of promoter Jack Kramer. A power hitter, he went on to success in the pros and is known for his intelligent TV tennis commentary. Seixas played in the Grand Masters at the 1974 Open looking extremely fit—conditioning was a great factor in his success—and young for his middle years.

Beginning in 1956, the Forest Hills finals were played without any American until Frank Froehling III faced Osuna and lost in 1963. Here is the way it went:

1956   Rosewall beat Hoad
1957   Anderson beat Cooper
1958   Cooper beat Anderson
1959   Fraser beat Olmedo (Peru)
1960   Fraser beat Laver
1961   Emerson beat Laver
1962   Laver beat Emerson
1963   Osuna (Mexico) beat Froehling (American)
1964   Emerson beat Stolle
1965   Santana (Spain) beat Drysdale (South Africa)
1966   Stolle beat Newcombe
1967   Newcombe beat Graebner (American)
1968   Ashe (American) beat Okker

The year 1968 brought the first Open and the beginning of a new era at Forest Hills. Looking at the names and forgetting the nationalities on the above list (all are Australian unless otherwise noted), you could not say that tennis itself at Forest Hills was in any decline. At least three on the list are among the all-time great players—Rosewall, Laver and Newcombe. And if America produced no one of this quality, the names of Richardson, MacKay, Flam, McKinley, Savitt, Ralston, and Riessen are those of top competitors. Ralston and McKinley in fact salvaged American honors in the 1963 Davis Cup 3–2 victory at Adelaide, Australia.

The one challenge round in the period at Forest Hills was in 1959, and this was the last time Davis Cup matches were played there. That challenge round was remarkable for the playing of Alejandro Olmedo on the U.S. team. Although from Peru, which had no Davis Cup team, Olmedo was an American college student at the University of Southern California and one of many outstanding Latin American players with inter-American ties—Segura and Fillol also come to mind. The Australians won 3–2 (the losing matches were lost by Laver!) and held the cup until Graebner and Ashe recovered it in 1968, and the United States held it for five years.

Rod Laver took the title only once at Forest Hills before turning pro, and it marked the first Grand Slam since Budge. He then came back in the second Open to win the second Grand Slam, the only player to win four major championships in a year two times. Of all the Australians Laver was and perhaps still is the greatest player even at thirty-six, although he has tapered off the competition. Whether he is the greatest player of all time is one of those endless arguments.

Laver won two Wimbledon titles before triumphing at Forest Hills. In the 1960 finals at the West Side he lost to Fraser, and the next year to Emerson. But in 1962, at the age of twenty-four, he took his first American title and made the Grand Slam by beating Emerson in four sets. Like Budge, he had deliberately set out to win the Grand Slam. When you ask him today what Forest Hills means to him, he replies automatically, "Why, the Grand Slam!"

The pressure this objective puts on you is what makes it such an exceptional honor. Anything along the way can spoil it—illness, injury, a bad call, an off day, exhaustion after a long semifinal. So when you have the three titles and you get to Forest Hills, the tension becomes one of your obstacles. And in this sense Forest Hills *is* the Grand Slam because it's the last of the championships, Australia being in winter, France and the United Kingdom in late spring and early summer.

In *The Education of a Tennis Player* (with Bud Collins, 1971) Laver recounts how a two-day New York rainfall increased this tension and forced him to indoor workouts that made his legs stiff. The Stadium court was so wet that it made the soggy balls feel like cantaloupes when he hit them.

His opponent was his old friend and rival Roy Emerson, whom he had beaten for the championship in Australia and France. But still he was so nervous that "I lost the feel of the racket completely." Whisky wrist, he calls this, and it comes from rushing your shots.

"You have to slow yourself down. Take a little more time. Release your grip between points. Put your racket in the other hand for a moment, and let your racket hand relax."

Slowing down included speeding up evidently, because he resolved to rush the net and avoid having to hit off grass. "You're crazy to let a ball land on a grass court most of the time, and at Forest Hills it's like dropping a baby out of a window: It may bounce nicely, but it isn't likely."

Emerson's famous foot dragging was causing him trouble, according to Laver's account, making it difficult to find a proper patch of grass to serve from because so much of the sod had been removed as he ripped it up. At any rate, in the fourth set Laver tipped the balance on service and on speed of foot. The last point was a top-spin lob, the only one Laver used that day. The crowd had been for Emmo, but they gave the redheaded Rocket a standing ovation, and Don Budge was there to greet him.

Now there was only the pro world to conquer, and Laver looked like another Budge, who had whipped the pros as soon as he started. Rod, though, was like the star college quarterback entering the pros and had a lot to learn, particularly from Ken Rosewall at Forest Hills in 1963 at the first pro tournament there in four years. A disappointing crowd saw a disappointing Laver and a super Rosewall. The little man with the fantastic backhand swept the Rocket away in straight sets in muggy weather.

In little more than an hour Laver had learned that not everyone thinks it's crazy to let a ball land on grass. Rosewall's ground strokes were too much for him and even Kenny's less baffling serve somehow was unreturnable time and again.

It took a little while after the debacle for Laver to prove his point—that he really was unbeatable. Gradually he rose to the top of the pro world, which brought him more than victory. He eventually became the game's first millionaire. In 1969 he repeated his Grand Slam, beating the undisputed best in the world. Thus he was unique, for Budge did not do it twice; nor did he have to face Vines and Perry the year he won his Grand Slam.

Tony Roche had beaten Gonzales in the fourth round, and taking the first set of the finals 9–7, it seemed for a moment he could win—but Laver finished him off 6–1, 6–3, 6–2, numbers that flashed electronically on a new $167,000 scoreboard above the marquee and beneath the sign COME TO MARLBORO COUNTRY. Laver earned $16,000 that historic day and proved that Forest Hills could live very well with Open tennis, and probably could not have survived without it.

He has not been a Forest Hills champion since for one reason or another, and he has lost matches. But he has won those that were critical to him. In 1971 he won thirteen straight from Rosewall, Newcombe, Roche, Emerson (twice), Ashe (twice), Okker (thrice), Taylor and Ralston (twice) on indoor courts to pile up $160,000 in less than two months. The Tennis Champions Classic, it was called.

The next year in the famous World Championship Tennis final in Moody Coliseum in Dallas, with twenty-one million people watching on TV, Laver suffered his biggest disappointment when Rosewall won in a five-set tie-breaker ending. Laver thinks this one match had much to do with the upsurge in tennis popularity in America.

Now a pro with his own tennis camp in New Hampshire, he relaxes a great deal and selects the events to play in to suit himself and maintain respectable earnings. Connors won $100,000 beating Laver in Las Vegas in the winter of 1975, but the aging Aussie still picked up $50,000 in TV and other fees, and Connors said it was the toughest match he had ever played.

The Australian surge eventually brought with it a new generation of women players, as those who watch World Team Tennis now will testify. But the women got started at least a decade later than the men, when Margaret Smith won the nationals at Forest Hills in 1965. But before that another non-American, who ranks with Connolly, Jacobs and the rest, Maria Bueno, of Brazil, appeared after Althea Gibson to become the first four-time titleholder since Alice Marble.

In Maria, Forest Hills had the best-looking champion of the era. Al Laney compared her to Suzanne Lenglen when she won the title the first time. "Not only is she the most graceful of all players but she uses every shot known to the game and all of the court," he wrote. Four years later Allison Danzig, a restrained writer, wrote of her winning performance against Margaret Smith as "one of the most electrifying bursts of super shot-making produced by a woman in the championship. . . . With the score 1–4 and 0–30 against her, Miss Bueno set the gallery wild with the dazzling strokes that stemmed from her racket."

A shot that was all her own was a running-blind backhand hit with her back to the net. She did this when a lob went over her head, and she hit it with such force that it would often win the point. Julie Heldman notes that the shot meant so much to Maria that if she failed to score it depressed her for several games thereafter.

Margaret Smith Court, who succeeded Maria as queen of the courts, is still a strong competitor and less a historical figure than a current one. She has run up five titles at Forest Hills, the most since Helen Wills won seven, and she has done it in the face of stiffer competition: Bueno, Billie Jean, Rosie Casals, Virginia Wade, Nancy Richey, Ann Haydon Jones, Evonne Goolagong and Chris Evert. The depth of good women players has never been greater than it is now, and it is increasing.

Margaret Court is a big woman—five feet nine inches—and plays the big game. In her native Australia they think of her in the same breath with Newcombe, Laver and Rosewall. At least one player, Marty Riessen, rates her as the greatest of all women who have played tennis. She probably is the best endowed physically, being one of those rare, perfect athletes with great strength, speed, coordination and tremendous determination. The Grand Slam is just one of her accomplishments, and she has won more major tournaments than any woman in history.

Moreover, Margaret is illness- and injury-proof. She did quit the game briefly in 1966 out of boredom, and childbirth kept her idle two seasons. Bobby Riggs's astonishing victory over her did nothing essentially to tarnish her luster, and fans are hoping to see her at Forest Hills in 1975. She could become a sort of Gonzales among women now that she has passed thirty and must face the younger players.

183

During the period preceding open tennis the game in America went through something of the same kind of doldrums observed in the first decade of the century, before Forest Hills was established. You can tell

Maria Bueno of Brazil was a four-time title-holder between 1959 and 1966.

Tony Trabert, while in the Navy, played for the American Davis Cup team in 1951. Two years later he won the singles at Forest Hills and repeated again in 1955. He helped Pat Somerall report the 1974 Open on CBS-TV.

Roy Emerson was one of the several Australians who put the U.S. players in the shade for more than ten years. He won two Forest Hills titles, 1961 and 1964, and dueled with Rod Laver as Tilden did with Johnston.

As if Forest Hills did not have enough glamour, the movie star Ginger Rogers used to add her charms to the scene (1950, here) during the nationals. The tag on her blouse assured her reentry to the clubhouse—as if she needed a pass!

from the size of the crowds at the finals of the nationals that there was a lack of enthusiasm for the sport that stands in such sharp contrast to today's strong support. Between 1959 and 1968, 1966 was the only year the Stadium was anywhere near full—Fred Stolle beat Newcombe that day. In 1960 only 7,000 were at the West Side finale to watch Fraser beat Laver.

In an effort to supplement its income the West Side Club arranged to have a number of rock concerts held in the Stadium. While they produced about $50,000 in revenue, the side effects made them short-lived. In one instance the Beatles landed on the lawn in a helicopter while fans pelted them with jelly beans—the rock group had been said to like jelly beans. For weeks lawnmowers were being gummed up by jelly beans that had been trampled into the grass courts. In another case a drugged performer had to be dragged into the Stadium to prevent a riot among fans he had kept waiting all night.

Then there was the security problem. Kids wanted to get into the clubhouse "to see how the rich folk live." And there was violence. When a

Australian tennis ascendency was no accident. These five hundred children in Sidney were rehearsing for an exhibition of "Strokemaking to Music" in 1957. It grated on American ears for years.

By 1971 American kids were making with their own jazzy racket work. Five years later the number of players in the country had tripled and Americans were winning again at Forest Hills.

scuffle outside the gate ended in a fatal knife fight, the club, deluged with complaints of neighbors about noise and disturbances on the streets of their quiet section, decided to terminate this experiment. It seems that tennis is the only thing the West Side is suited for. Even the use of the Stadium for Easter-morning services in the late forties was short-lived.

But if tennis was to prosper, something had to happen to it in this country. The USLTA under Louis Carruthers of the West Side had endorsed the concept of open tournaments in the thirties, but the International Lawn Tennis Federation in Paris was determined that this would never happen. The ILTF response to the USLTA's reassertion of its belief in open tennis in 1960 was as adamant as ever. It was as though nothing had happened since the days of the Four Musketeers. The hypocrisy of paying amateurs—"I once got $4,500 for expenses as an amateur," Rosie Casals told a reporter in 1970—was simply ignored.

By coincidence open tennis was inaugurated in Paris (because Wimbledon forced the issue) in May 1968, at the very time when students rioted in resentment of the blindness of an older generation.

187

Forest Hills always provides suspense. The master of that genre in films, Alfred Hitchcock, came to the Davis Cup matches in 1950 and shot footage for his picture Strangers on a Train. He chats here with publicity man Charles Brandt.

Victor Seixas was a dogged retriever. This quality finally won him the title in 1954.

188

21

OPEN AND UNHYPOCRITICAL TENNIS

"Tennis is big enough and broad enough for both the true amateur and professional," Ned Potter wrote in *Kings of the Court*.

The word *open* means open to all competitors, amateur and professional, but it has overtones of an openness badly needed in tennis, which had become enclosed by a stubborn complacency born of its very success. Had not the players forced the issue, the associations would have been content to remain like the colleges which blithely act as farm clubs for professional football teams under the aloof banner of amateurism. Forest Hills would have continued to be the arena where the amateur was blooded for professional competition elsewhere.

Who would deny that amateurism touches a deeper human chord than professionalism? To train and compete merely for the sake of the game requires a selfless spiritual commitment for young people who wish to test their powers. When tennis was played by a wealthy few it had the quality of a schoolboy contest. But it quickly developed into something else, and if no one got rich off it, there were benefits to be derived in the form of expenses, and connections that led to jobs.

Bill Tilden was one of the great freeloaders of tennis. In 1926 Tom Pettit, the famous pro at the Newport Casino, said that if he had known how much money there was in amateur tennis, he would have remained an amateur. The term *tennis bum* is attributed by Parke Cummings to George Lott, who coined it after turning pro.

Until the sixties no one got rich as an amateur. Vines turned pro because in the Depression he could not support a wife on the expenses he earned on the circuit. But in the so-called go-go years it was possible to earn $50,000 and still be an amateur.

The historical context, it will be remembered, was one of national torment over Vietnam. In this atmosphere the counterculture surfaced in the Free Speech Movement, student sit-ins, bizarre clothing, hippies, pornography, swinging sexual mores, Women's Lib, flower children who smoked grass. The Establishment shuddered, swayed but did not topple. Among institutions attacked were organized sports.

We have had only one American Revolution. Other revolts have simply been absorbed and their desirable features appropriated by the status quo. And so we saw some rich tennis players and still see them in humble jeans. There is a picture of Marty Riessen walking down the Champs Elysées with Arthur Ashe in just such garb in Riessen's engaging book *Match Point* (with Richard Evans, 1973). Riessen in fact embodies the revolution that led to adoption of the open concept.

A Midwestern college basketball player, Riessen was as square as they come by his own description and played the tennis circuit without a thought of going pro. "It was hard work being a shamateur," he wrote, "lugging all that loot around." He would have to carry a color TV set off the court as his prize. Cash piled up as players toured the world. Ray Ruffels, an Australian Davis Cup player, lost $4,000 to a thief in Iran. (He later managed to wheedle $2,000 out of the Shah!)

By 1967 things were at a low ebb. Davis Cup players earned $28 a day during matches and $20 when not playing. They trained five hours a day. And that year the United States team lost to tiny Ecuador. Riessen claims the USLTA paid Emerson and Stolle $1,000 each five weeks to play the Eastern circuit. Marty turned pro, concluding that he liked the good life as well as any man. "There is not much that South Orange, New Jersey, has in common with Cannes on the Cote d'Azur," he said.

It is not an attitude that old-timers who played the circuit for room, board and other expenses can adopt as their own. But as influential members of the USLTA, they put up surprisingly little resistance to open tournaments when the test came. The West Side had always wanted some open tennis. Its president, Renville McMann, had taken up the open cause in the late fifties where Carruthers had left off twenty years before.

As the head of the USLTA, he appointed a committee under Perry Jones, Southern California's ruling power, to formulate an open program, which they did, only to be turned down by the executive committee. In Paris the International Lawn Tennis Federation would have authorized open tournaments in 1960 but for the fact, according to Will Grimsley of the AP, that the necessary proxy votes were in the pocket of a delegate in the men's room. For eight more years the hypocrisy continued, buoyed by the pressure of one man's bladder.

Meanwhile the pros were getting better organized. The formula of pro tennis had been that of a series of exhibition matches. Tournaments were held occasionally but they were not regularly successful because they lacked the kind of continuing buildup provided by a circuit always in the news. The USLTA and other national associations controlled the tournaments through their member clubs who had the best facilities. Forest Hills Stadium was the site of a so-called world championship pro tournament in 1963 that was so poorly attended no prize money was distributed— not even to Rosewall, the winner.

However, in 1964 Edward Hickey, the public relations director of New England Merchants National Bank, was jolted when his fourteen-year-old daughter said it was silly not to let Rod Laver come back to Longwood for the national doubles just because he turned pro. Why not, he wondered, sponsor a good pro tournament at Longwood after a series of tournaments across the country that would comprise a national pro circuit? With the help of Jack Kramer, who had given up the one-night-stand business, Hickey created eight tournaments with $10,000 purses for sixteen players. Ten years later Longwood's U.S. Pro Championship had gained a particular distinction by being scheduled just before the Open at Forest Hills and thereby attracting many of the top players in a sort of preliminary tournament, drawing 10,000 people a day in double sessions.

At the same time the British Lawn Tennis Association was trying to beat down the conservatism of the ILTF that came in part from small countries which feared that open tennis would drain away players from their tournaments. Added conservative support came from a shift of sentiment at the top of the USLTA. The British, though, grew liberal. With all its old prestige, Wimbledon was not getting the best tennis because so much of it was not professional. The British were fed up with the ILTF.

During the August bank holiday in 1967 a pro tournament was held at Wimbledon for the first time. Laver, beating Rosewall in straight sets, took home $8,400. The All-England Club management muttered something about the hope of making this an annual event. "We shall have more to say in about three months." It took less.

On October 5, 1967, after the playing season was over, the BLTA council voted for an open Wimbledon, and two months later this was officially approved. All players in England thereafter became indistinguishable as amateurs or pros and were simply to be called players. This abandonment of the amateur category was not acceptable to the USLTA, which supported the open idea in its February meeting in Coronado, California, but maintained the distinction between pro and amateur players. One of the important votes was cast by Henry Benisch of the West Side, representing the Eastern section. Of seventeen sections only the Southwest was in opposition.

The ILTF was now forced to go along, and in March twelve open

Rod Laver was the second man to win the Grand Slam (after Budge). He won it first in 1962 and repeated the feat in 1969, as shown here. Laver, the game's first millionaire, did not play in the 1974 Open, but shrewdly accepted Jimmy Connors's $100,000 challenge match in February 1975. Youth won, but Laver soothed any bruised pride with a $60,000 loser's share.

tournaments were sanctioned for 1968, with the distinction between pro and amateur player categories retained. For a time this little semantic difference allowed the amateur associations to keep a certain number of registered players, considered separate from the pros under contract to promoters.

A history of Forest Hills is not the vehicle for recounting the ensuing wrangles that open tennis led to. To oversimplify events, as in the original French Revolution of 1789, lawyers came to determine much of what went on for the next several years. And as in the New Deal, a host of initials came to stand for powerful new bureaucracies: the World Championship Tennis group of millionaire oil scion Lamar Hunt, WCT; the Association of Tennis Professionals, ATP; and later, World Team Tennis, WTT. These clashed repeatedly with the *ancien régime,* which invoked the one power it knew, suspension, only to be met by the greater force players always exercised individually and now could use as a group—not entering a tournament. En masse this became boycott. Wimbledon was boycotted in 1972 by the ATP. Pilic was suspended by the ILTF for refusing to play on the Yugoslav Davis Cup team in 1973. Connors was not allowed to play in the 1974 French Championships because he played World Team Tennis.

For anyone who cared, organized tennis, which had been carried on without visible conflict by well-meaning but nonetheless autocratic patrons in the amateur associations, was being exposed to bitter controversy that was too difficult for the public to follow. In fact, a sort of anarchy reigned for several years while the pros, divided into rival groups under so many warlords, worked out their own *modus vivendi* and the money poured much oil on troubled waters.

By 1970 Gene Scott, writing in *World Tennis,* was able to identify five power groups: Lamar Hunt, Fred Podesta, the USLTA, Donald Dell and Bill Riordan (who manages Jimmy Connors). Another group of importance, Scott pointed out, was the International Players Association, which has fifty members and is headed by John Newcombe. The problem facing these entities was to coordinate dates to see that various tournaments had sufficient gate-drawing stars.

So amateur associations like the USLTA had lost considerable bargaining power when open tennis came in, but they gained the participation of the great pros in their events, and that brought revenues which allowed them to strengthen their organizations and sponsor wider development of tennis in their countries.

Lava flows faster than a tennis association can move to change its ways. In 1968 the first Open was held at Forest Hills. But to prove something or other, a national amateur tournament preceded this event at Longwood. Arthur Ashe, Jr., won both events.

The unanticipated success of the first black tournament player since Althea Gibson was one of the happiest things that ever occurred in tennis. Tennis now had its Jackie Robinson or its Bill Russell. The 1967 finals between Newcombe and Graebner had drawn only 10,000. As Ashe faced the wiry Dutchman, Tom Okker, the Stadium was filled to overflowing. No American had won the championship since Trabert won it in 1955. Ashe was the official champion already, but Forest Hills was the real test. The pros had been eliminated, including Ashe's mentor, Gonzales. Okker, strictly speaking, was what they called "a registered player," a status that allowed him to compete as an amateur and still take prize money. So Ashe, the strict amateur, holder of the U.S. amateur title, turned down the $14,000 first prize for winning the Open, and Okker, the loser, accepted the check!

Handsome, willowy and with a serve almost as fast as that of Gonzales in his prime, Ashe had made the Davis Cup team in 1963, and in 1969 he won two singles matches against Mexico, but he was unable to get Army leave to play at Forest Hills that year. Naturally, with Laver, New-

Australia's Margaret Smith Court has to rank as one of the best to win the title at Forest Hills, which she did in 1965, 1970, 1971 and 1973.

England has a strong competitor in Virginia Wade, who won the first U.S. Open finals over Billie Jean King. Teamed with Margaret Court, she won the doubles in 1969 and 1973.

combe, Rosewall and Roche in the 1968 Open, Ashe was not expected to win. How did it happen?

A loving parent and a dedicated patron-coach, and a great tennis star all helped this gifted youth to develop into one of the game's great players. His widowed father, a Richmond policeman, was a religious man who ran a harmonious home and taught his two sons patience. The late Dr. Robert W. Johnson of Lynchburg, the black tennis patron and football player known as Whirlwind Johnson, who coached Althea Gibson, took the talented Arthur as a prospect for bigger things, training his eye by making him hit a ball on a string with a broomstick.

Arthur did all the things young players do, won tournaments and got ranked, until at eighteen he was twenty-eighth nationally among men players. At UCLA, which gave him a scholarship, he met Pancho Gonzales, who sharpened his game so that by 1963 he could win the National Hard Court title. Five years later, at twenty-five, he was the champion.

Of course Arthur's career was a more lonely one than most players have. Being black, he was either the victim of discrimination, curiosity or a friendliness that was patronizing. After winning the amateur national grasscourt title at Longwood, he said that he was effectively barred from membership at seven eighths of U.S. clubs. It is not in his nature to be an agitator, but in his determined way he has added strength to the civil rights movement, particularly in his sensible stand against apartheid and *for* South African tennis. He maintains that blacks are kept out of competitive tennis in America not just by discrimination but by economics. It is not a game that will flourish in the ghetto.

The first Open at Forest Hills was a tremendous success. The mix of amateur and pro, the appearance of color in tennis clothing, the use of metal rackets, the commercial spirit of the event—all announced a new beginning at the same old stand. The professional spirit, instead of cheapening the game, as it had been feared, enlivened it. Tennis became the new enterprise to be exploited by every means, and ironically the boom that produces higher tournament revenues is making it possible for amateur associations to do a better job than when they were completely in the saddle.

One of the best books on tennis was written about Ashe's semifinal victory over Graebner. In *Levels of the Game,* John McPhee says he was impressed by what he saw of Forest Hills as a place. "It must have cost at least two hundred thousand dollars to produce this scene," he wrote, adding, "The players themselves paid their way to Forest Hills for this match, though—20 cents a piece on the subway."

The very next year the USLTA beefed up its salaried staff. It was an embattled organization, openly attacked by players and their representatives. Donald Dell, for example, boasted that under him in 1968 and 1969 the Davis Cup teams had earned $175,000 for the USLTA, a passé organization in his view that was not promoting the game as much as the promoters were.

Forest Hills itself became a forum and a marketplace where players and promoters sounded off and made big deals. In 1970, in the women's locker room of the West Side Tennis Club, an *ad hoc* group aided by Gladys Heldman, then publisher of *World Tennis* magazine, successfully organized against Jack Kramer and obtained bigger prize money for women from the Pacific Southwest Tournament in Los Angeles. This led to the Virginia Slims circuit that gave women pros a world of their own.

Forest Hills eventually became part of the Grand Prix system, which has brought probably the most sensible formula to a chaotic situation. It is the old Eastern-circuit idea on a worldwide scale played for big money. Points are awarded to contestants according to the importance of the event, and a championship playoff determines each year's winner. The player with the most points also picks up a $100,000 bonus. In 1974 twenty-two-year-old Guillermo Vilas of Argentina emerged as the top Grand Prix player, with earnings of $119,844 and a visibility that put him in a class with Connors. In that year Connors won $285,490 in prize money around the world. Newcombe won $248,230, Vilas $226,110 and Borg $200,160. Nine others won over $100,000.

The chief value to the organized tennis of the Grand Prix, which is efficiently run by the British insurance firm Commercial Union, is the constant publicity and TV exposure it brings. The tie-in with amateur-association events eliminates the conflict between the amateur associations and the pros.

Forest Hills—that is, the West Side Club—gets no money from the Grand Prix, but rather contributes $15,000 in exchange for being a Class A event to which players will be attracted by the number of points they can earn.

The Open has changed Forest Hills—for the better. The older players have no sentimental attachment to the place, which they compare with the more spacious and ceremonial Wimbledon. But the public seems more enthralled than ever, judging from the crowds. The change to clay courts has brought with it predictions that now the West Side is just one more club, lacking in distinction, and letters are written to *The New York Times* warning that the Open will move to California.

The end of grass was foreseen as early as 1969 by Charles Tucker, the club's Open chairman in 1974, who observed that it then cost $50,000 a year to maintain grass courts the players no longer want. With clay Forest Hills will still be unique because of its stadium and proximity to midtown, and the eighth U.S. Open will have a new dimension with a slow surface most of the pros prefer to grass. The prospect of a Vilas–Connors final is in the Forest Hills tradition. The fact that both are pros at such a young age adds to the glamour of such an event.

Art Buchwald has a few words after playing with Senator Kennedy during the Robert F. Kennedy Celebrity Tournament held at Forest Hills a week before the U.S. Open.

22

THE RAPE OF THE LAWN

Visitors to the West Side Tennis Club in the winter of 1975 were witnesses to a historic transformation. Bulldozers, piles of gravel and drainage pipe lay on what had once been the lawn outside the Stadium. Inside the deep green surface had been replaced by the pastel green of Har-tru, a clay with a grainy texture produced by a very fine crushed stone. Gone was more than half the sod on which generations of the world's greatest players had struggled.

To many people, perhaps to most, the shift from grass to clay seemed a dreadful mistake, yielding to the overbearing demands of professional athletes grown too powerful for the good of the game. To some West Side members the decision to tear out acres of precious grass nurtured with so much care and cost was so devastating that they got a restraining order to delay the work of the contractor, Philip Lagana and Son, Inc. It was soon vacated, however, by a superior court, and all that the dissident members have to show to vindicate their obstruction is the fact that the vote to put down clay for the 1975 Open was actually opposed by a majority of members present at the special meeting and carried only by virtue of proxies.

"The membership was not informed," said a spokesman of the *ad hoc* committee fighting the change. "Had they known the facts, we'd still have grass."

The facts as some see them are that the West Side Tennis Club could have defied the USLTA and insisted on remaining, along with Wimbledon and the clubs of Australia, one of the big international lawn tennis centers. When the USLTA explained that the players would force the Open to be put on in some other city, the question came back: "What other city has the facilities to give you the gate receipts you get in New York?" These people believe that the USLTA was bluffing. Even if the Open had been held elsewhere, the club could have put on its own grass tournament and called it the Forest Hills Open. So went the argument.

But the club is not powerful enough to withstand the force of both the players and the amateur association, which is a national body. The sentiment for grass is Eastern. California and Texas—and Illinois, for that matter—were never part of the swanky grass circuit and resent the continued domination of the championships by New York. That any other section will come up with the money to build a facility clearly superior to Forest Hills, though, is unlikely in the present economic climate. Reluctantly, the Board of Governors of the West Side gave in to the USLTA after a delaying action of two years.

What makes the decision look like weakness in some eyes is that the USLTA negotiated a new three-year contract with CBS for $1 million, of which the West Side will get nothing. Previously the club got half the TV rights, but the sum of money was only $150,000. The club, on the other hand, has to pay only half the bill for the new courts, which will cost close to $225,000. And it will still get half the Open gate receipts, which are bound to be higher if a proposal to install lights in the Stadium can be made acceptable to local residents. Night tennis promises to fill the Stadium a second time in a single day, with two separate admission charges. Longwood doubled its crowds with night matches and even put on the finals of the U.S. Pro Championships under the lights on a weekday in 1974.

A USLTA official said, "Don't feel sorry for the West Side Tennis Club. They're doing all right." His remark is borne out by the fact that there is a discussion of improving the clubhouse facilities, particularly the meager women's locker room. And the club is bound to save money by having fewer grass courts to take care of. There will still be eight lawn-tennis courts for members to play on, and because they do not have to be maintained for tournament play, a procedure that made them playable only three or four days a week, and because none of the grass courts will be used in the Open, members may get in just as much lawn playing as ever.

Furthermore the new clay courts increase playing time because they dry more quickly. There had been thirty-six courts. Now there will be forty-seven. From the spectators' point of view the clay setup will be better to watch because the layout will allow room for temporary grandstands. Forest Hills will be a more comfortable place to watch tennis at, and there will be additional toilet facilities and drinking fountains. The clubhouse courts, which the players disliked because of the noise from the veranda, will remain grass and will therefore not be used for tournament events.

And the players ought to be happier on clay than on grass. But not necessarily. Billie Jean King has expressed concern that the women's game will not be the crowd pleaser it was on grass. The men would rather have

199

a hard surface. But the West Side already had too many clay courts to consider putting in concrete or other variants of artificial tennis courts. The members are used to clay, which is cooler and easier on the feet.

A bizarre compromise may be possible. Bill Talbert, who runs the Open, flew to New Orleans to look at some golf greens covered with a surface called Mod Sod, developed by the golfer Fred Haas. It is an artificial fiber, like Astroturf, on which sand is sprinkled. The color looks a bit washed out, but the surface seems to play well and is cooler than Astroturf or asphalt. It rests on a clay base. The only such court in existence has been installed on the Burns Street side of the clubhouse in Forest Hills, next to the bubble that is put up in winter.

The veneration for real sod will not die lightly. One club member, who lives in Forest Hills and agrees with the decision to go to clay yet regrets it at the same time, asked Owney Sheridan, the grounds keeper, if he could have some pieces of the grass as a memento. So he filled up the trunk of his car and took the rich turf home and planted it in his garden.

The tennis patch at the edge of his own lawn was a much deeper green and of course more finely sown, and his wife, gazing at it, frowned. "It looks like a grave," said she.

"It is," said he, who had probably played many sets on that very bit of turf. "I want to be buried under it."

The removal of the grass probably would never have happened if the top tournaments had not gone professional. Clay may be taken for a symbol of the new world of competition tennis in which more clashes occur off court than on. That Jimmy Connors could sue Jack Kramer for $10 million because Kramer allegedly is running a monopolistic players' union, the Association of Tennis Professionals, that kept him out of tournaments and affected his earnings, tells us how far down the road to riches the game has come. Björn Borg has won so much money at the age of nineteen that he has moved to Monte Carlo to avoid the high taxation of Scandinavia. The top players earn several hundred thousand dollars a year. The shamateurs were perhaps dishonest, but at least they were for the most part poor and they kept quiet.

"The USLTA now spends most of its time on a hundred and fifty pros instead of on the public, for whom it should develop tennis," an official said. "For most people it's more fun to help run tournaments for the glamorous Amritraj brothers and Ilie Nastase than it is to put together the kind of program Eve Kraft ran in Princeton, where she had the whole town running around with rackets."

And like it or not, without the tournaments there would be no USLTA. Its major revenue continues to come from Forest Hills. For a while the USLTA dreamed of building the Open up to a half million attendance under the guidance of Owen Williams, a South African promoter hired in 1969. But tennis is something of a family, and it was found to be more economical to turn the Open over to one of its old members, Billy Talbert, who at no charge to the USLTA has been that event's chief executive since 1970.

This arrangement underscores the fact that tennis, for all the hoopla and big money, is a cameo sport by comparison with football, baseball, hockey, basketball or horse racing. Here it is, the biggest event in American tennis, and it's run on a volunteer basis out of the office of a printing executive on the lower West Side of Manhattan. The Open is not the Rose Bowl game. Ella Musolino, Talbert's capable assistant, handles the details, and he handles, or tries to handle, the players.

As a man who was Davis Cup captain for five years, he knows the players, yet they baffle him. After the 1974 Open he got only one letter of thanks from a player. Favors done for wealthy pros receive no acknowledgment. The job is a headache, but it must have its compensations. Talbert likes people and is thick-skinned enough not to be bothered by the incessant demands made by promoters, the press, the umpires, ball boys and spectators. He says he wishes someone would fire him, but who else would take this work on without charge? And who else could answer the question from the Lighthouse for the Blind: Can we put on a match between George Plimpton and John Lindsay to promote our cause during the Open? He knows when he can schedule such a match because he has been doing it for so long. Remember that the Open is not one tournament but ten: men's singles, women's singles, men's thirty-five singles, grand masters, men's doubles, women's doubles, mixed doubles, senior doubles, junior boys' singles, junior girls' singles.

One of the biggest innovations Talbert brought to the Open was the tie breaker, which was developed by Newport's James Van Alen, the originator of the VASSS system—Van Alen Simplified Scoring System. It is controversial among the players, but it caught on with the public because it prevented sets from dragging on beyond thirteen games. At 6–6 the tie breaker begins, a five-out-of-nine-point coda with serves going alternately 2-2-2-3. The ninth point is sudden death. At Wimbledon the tie breaker goes to 13 points. But whatever the merits of the long set, they belong to a more leisurely era when there was no TV.

For the eighth Open Talbert has persuaded the city at last to recognize an event that surely has given New York enough good publicity over the years to offset some of the bad. Of course there are few votes to be had at Forest Hills. The only politicians you are likely to see there are federal officials presenting trophies. Both Nixon and Agnew as vice-presidents presented trophies at Forest Hills, but no president of the United States has ever appeared there while in office. Tom Dewey came once while he was governor. Now the privilege of awarding checks and trophies is claimed by executives of the firms helping to sponsor the Open. In keeping these business people happy, Talbert has been able to bring enough money in to avoid a ticket-price increase since he took charge.

London, incidentally, subsidizes Wimbledon in many ways, providing free security, added bus service, and much promotion for the national fortnight.

23

TALENT UNLIMITED

OPEN TENNIS IS JUST EIGHT YEARS OLD. In this short time an enormous number of highly talented players has appeared, and some people question whether there is as much quality in the game as in the amateur days. This is another argument that can never be settled, but it would be difficult to maintain that there is very much mediocrity among the top twenty pros. What is responsible for the quantitative increase is the widening of the player pool through internationalization.

The Soviet Union, for example, is just beginning a development program to extend beyond the bureaucratic elite—or perhaps to enlarge the number of players in the elite. The USLTA welcomes the competition. So far as tennis is concerned, there has never been a cold war.

Forest Hills pushed for wider foreign-player participation in the nationals during the sixties. It used to be that foreign players were classified as such and seeded separately. Internationalization made this segregation ludicrous. In 1962 funds were privately raised around New York by Colonel Edward P. Eagan's People-to-People Sports Committee to fly players from thirty-five countries to play at Forest Hills. At the time there was a flap over this gesture, which looked to some like a form of payment to the amateur foreigners. Now many of the players from abroad make enough money to bring their families on their American tournament tours.

Even an average player can earn $30,000 to $40,000 a year, but he must play thirty to forty tournaments and put in four or five hours a day on the court to stay in the competition. The U.S. Open is not the most lucrative event, despite the gross, but it is *the* event to play in for prestige. The national tournaments, particularly in England, France, Australia and the United States, are focal points where big-time tennis comes together in meaningful climaxes.

"Remember Forest Hills '71, the year of Chrissie Evert . . . ?" begins an article in *World Tennis.*

People remember Forest Hills. They are unlikely to remember the many Grand Prix events, the CBS Classics, the Virginia Slims tournaments. There are so many events now that tennis is like any other sport, a confusing blend of impressions that come into focus on climactic occasions—the Super Bowl, the World Series, the Stanley Cup playoffs, the Kentucky Derby.

The seven Opens at Forest Hills are really too recent to be historic. They belong to a review of current events. Here a roll calling of the players who have distinguished themselves at Forest Hills since 1968 must suffice.

After Arthur Ashe won the first Open in 1968, Rod Laver came back in 1969 to Forest Hills to beat his Australian friend Tony Roche easily after dropping the first set 7–9. Thus Rod holds two Forest Hills championships, which seems to be the quota in the men's singles now. No one since Fred Perry has held the title three times. You can say this is because the pros were excluded until 1968 and that Budge or Gonzales could have gone on like Tilden, but since the pros have been included this just has not happened. No one has yet won the Open men's singles twice. This is a nice goal for Jimmy Connors to shoot for, and he could even be the man to become the fixture Tilden was if he cared to.

Roche got to the finals again in 1970 but lost to Rosewall after winning the first set. This was the year of the tie breaker, and the third set went to Kenny 7–6. Rosewall got to the finals again four years later with such disastrous consequences that he too will no doubt have to settle for two Forest Hills titles, won fourteen years apart—an unusual time span between championships. He played a finals in 1954, losing to Trabert, making his total of finals at Forest Hills four.

Stan Smith, a Californian transplanted to South Carolina and the leading American after Ashe, won the title in 1971 against Jan Kodes, the tenacious Czech and Wimbledon champion, taking the fourth set on a tie breaker. Kodes that year made the famous remark "Playing on grass is a joke." The handsome six-foot four-inch blond Smith has a big mustache, a quiet, unflamboyant personality and a tremendous serve. His victory came the same year as Billie Jean King's first Open title to give the Americans their first Forest Hills sweep in sixteen years. Ranked number one in 1973, he was disappointing in 1974, possibly because he had played too much tennis. He married Marjorie Gengler, a Princeton tennis star, in the fall of 1974.

Ilie Nastase, the Rumanian, has enormous talent and of course is most

Earl Bucholz

204

Arthur Ashe

All fall down! A portfolio of Stadium pratfalls guaranteed not to be seen on clay:

Pauline Betz

Ken Rosewall

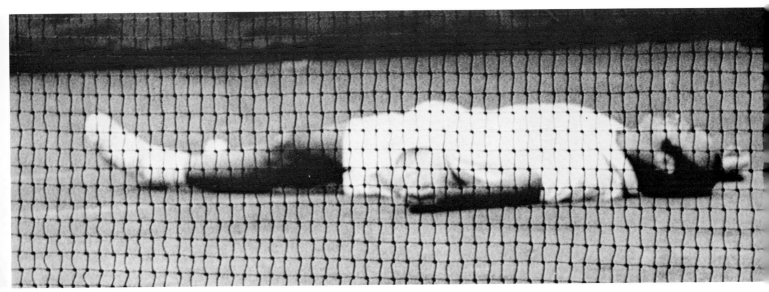

Andres Gimeno

With folded arms, Owney Sheridan, Forest Hills' grounds keeper, talks with the author.

206 *Backgammon is the players' second game. Roscoe Tanner, in the dotted shirt, plays in the clubhouse men's lounge between matches.*

This lovely young spectator is probably watching her husband, Ilie Nastase, at the 1974 Open.

207

She was Billie Jean Moffitt when this picture was taken. She began winning at Forest Hills in 1967 and continued in 1971, 1972 and 1974. Her concentration is something!

famous for his temper tantrums, which have earned him the sobriquet "Nasty." Just how much of this is a put-on no one can say, but he is an uneven performer. In 1972 he was at the top of his form and beat Arthur Ashe in five sets. Two years later he did not reach the quarterfinals and succumbed in five sets to Roscoe Tanner, who has one of the game's biggest serves, big enough to beat Smith in four sets before Connors mastered him in three.

John Newcombe, the last Forest Hills amateur titleholder, won the Open in 1973 against Kodes in five sets. This popular, smiling Australian, who has grown the biggest mustache in the game, earned a second seeding in 1974 but could not overcome old Kenny Rosewall in the semifinals, thus upsetting predictions of a Connors–Newcombe final. He turned thirty-one in May 1975, not too old to win the title—Rosewall won it at thirty-six —but there is Connors, not to mention a new cast of players: Vilas, Borg,

Amritraj, Ramirez, Metreveli, Stockton, Gerulaitis, Orantes, and the youngsters Martin and Taygan. Others who have sparkled during the period of the Open include Riessen, Graebner, Gorman, Okker, Pasarell and El Shafei.

The Open has brought the national doubles championship to Forest Hills, after a long monopoly by Longwood. Smith and Lutz won it in 1968 and 1974, and Newcombe has been a titlist twice—in 1971 with Roger Taylor of Great Britain and in 1973 with Owen Davidson. Other winning teams have been: 1969, Rosewall–Stolle; 1970, Barthes–Pilic; 1972, Drysdale–Taylor.

On the women's side of the Open, after Virginia Wade beat Billie Jean King in 1968, the titles have been won three times each by King and Margaret Smith Court. Chris Evert has not yet won the title, but give her time. In 1971 she appeared at sixteen with her pigtails and two-handed backhand and a string of victories behind her like a young prize-fighter and took over the Stadium, the standout of the tournament. Billie Jean did beat her in straight sets in the semifinals. With Chrissie gone, several hundred fewer than the 13,000 who watched her lose showed up to see Billie Jean take Rosie Casals for the title in three sets.

In 1973 Billie Jean, feeling ill, had to default in something of a pet in the fourth round to Julie Heldman, and Margaret Court beat Evonne Goolagong in three sets for the championship. It looked like Evonne might take the cup in 1974 after beating Chrissie 6–0, 6–7, 6–3. At the time Chrissie was setting most of the headlines because she had won at Wimbledon and had presumably won Jimmy Connors's heart. King remained queen in a fantastic finale after being down 0–3 in the third set with a crowd rooting for the lovely Australian.

That unchivalrous support of a foreigner may have been Evonne's undoing, because it made Billie Jean just mad enough to dig in and win a match as good as any ever seen at the West Side Stadium. Despite this masterful performance, King was rated second to Evert by *World Tennis* magazine on the basis of overall tournament performance during 1974.

With Margaret Court coming back in 1975 after having a baby, it will be interesting to see if Chrissie can finally take the title playing on clay, the surface she is best on. Other contenders include the Russian Morozova, Melville, Casals, Heldman, Hunt, Gunter, and Wade, with Nagelson, Durr, Navratilova, Overton and Stove adding competition. Evert, King, Goolagong and Court, however, are the standouts.

In the women's doubles Margaret Court has been an Open titlist four times. Her partners have been Maria Bueno in 1968, Virginia Wade in 1969 and 1973, and Judy Dalton in 1970. Dalton won with Casals in 1971. Françoise Durr and Betty Stove won in 1972 and 1974.

What lies ahead for women's tennis is an increasing number of good players. Between Billie Jean King's promotion of women's sports and the opening up of athletics in general to girls in the schools, the next decade should see a gradual increase in the number of entries at Forest Hills in women's singles and doubles—and possibly in mixed doubles competition.

24

THE SPIRIT
OF THE WEST SIDE

THE WEST SIDE TENNIS CLUB, by remaining small (850 active members), has carried on pretty much as it did from the time it settled in Forest Hills in 1913. For all the attention the great matches have drawn to the club, its members are individually self-effacing and not anxious for publicity. They are happy to let the name players talk to the press, and shrewdly realize that the less visibility the club has as a club, the less of a target it will be.

The club is run by a thirteen-man board of governors headed in 1975 by the president, Eugene F. Brady, an attorney. Traditionally the vice-president becomes president. Currently, insurance man Charles W. Tucker, Jr., is vice-president and chairman of the important U.S. Open committee.

Every year the club issues a small booklet listing members, past presidents, club champions and grounds and house rules. The one rule that catches the eye today is Rule 11:

> All players shall wear white tennis shoes without heels, spikes or pegs, and players shall not appear in the club house or the club grounds or courts in tennis apparel including outer sweaters that are not white or off-white in color; provided, however, that women players may, at their individual discretion, wear light pastel outer sweaters, and pastel or brightly colored accessories such as narrow

belts and hair ribbons; and outer sweaters worn both by men and women may have colored trim around collar and cuffs if desired. While it is preferred that this rule be followed at all times, it is nevertheless suspended at such times during the months of November through April only, when due to weather conditions it may be impractical to follow this rule.

That such a regulation should appear in 1974 when sports fashions rule out no color combination and Billie Jean King favors blue sneakers is a tribute to tradition and the fond wish that change can be resisted when it is not for the better. The reluctance to allow even winter weather to alter the decorum that is surely one of the pleasures of good tennis is in the West Side spirit of excellence in all things. After all, Forest Hills claimed championship tennis partly on the grounds that the display of women's dresses at Newport were a distraction.

Rule 11 has not caused anyone in a scarlet warm-up suit to be thrown off a West Side court. It simply is a reminder of an old standard.

The club also shows great respect for its own past, and lists the names of members who joined forty or more years ago. Of the thirty-seven currently in this category, the first is Walter Merrill Hall, who joined in 1909, four years prior to the move to Forest Hills.

Now eighty-seven, Hall still recalls historic moments in the game vividly. When asked about the time he had Tilden at match point and lost a lob in the sun, he is quick to correct the questioner:

"I did not have Tilden at match point. This was in 1918 in the quarter-finals. I remember the lob well. It was questionable whether the lob would actually go over the net, but it did—and without touching the tape. Then it bounced very high and I simply could not see the ball in the sun. I waved my racket at it but never touched the ball. Tilden's real escape was the day before, when I had him two sets to one and three-love in the fourth set. It began to rain, and the referee called us off the court at three-two. The next day the sun shone and Tilden won."

That year Hall was ranked fourth in the country. He later became president of the USLTA as well as of the West Side, but his greatest distinction was to have been chairman of the USLTA Davis Cup committee from 1937 to 1951. During his tenure two West Side Club members were captains. The United States held the cup six out of nine times in that period (there was no competition during World War II).

Hall was good enough to win the club doubles championship when he was forty-six. As an observer of today's game, he has seen no essential change in the style of play. "It began with McLoughlin," he said in an interview. "A hard serve and speed of foot that get you to the net, that's the American game. Australia adopted it. Laver plays the same way they played fifty years ago."

Ralph B. Gatcomb, a veteran who joined the club in 1910, was club doubles champion the year after Hall lost to Tilden. Gatcomb once took a set from Tilden on the boards of the Seventh Regiment Armory during a

National Indoor tournament. He was president of the West Side from 1949 to 1951, and remembers the storm that knocked the stone eagle off the Stadium into what he called "Agutter's court," where the club pro, George Agutter, gave lessons.

This episode, which occurred while Althea Gibson was playing Louise Brough, recalled Gatcomb's friendship with Althea. "She had never played on grass when I first met her, so I arranged with Sarah Palfrey for her to play at the West Side. I also found housing for her during tournaments."

Gatcomb can also remember what happened to some of the turf brought to Forest Hills from 238th Street. "When the Stadium was built in 1923, that old turf was moved again and put down inside the Stadium. That was what they tore out last fall to make way for clay," he said—with a sense of real loss. He does not approve of the changeover to clay.

"It was good sod, but our grass was overplayed during the tournaments. We had an agronomist from Rutgers who took soil samples and said we had excellent conditions for grass." The Japanese beetles apparently agreed. Gatcomb has vivid recollections of plagues of ants, beetles and crabgrass.

Gatcomb is an admirer of Bobby Riggs, who he thinks has been wrongly characterized by the press as a tightwad. "He put his own money into a losing pro championship at Forest Hills in 1961 and was honest enough to tell Jack Kramer that if he would put up $1,500 he couldn't lose more than half of it. When I said this was a strange way to raise money, Bobby answered that it was the truth, and he wasn't going to promise what he couldn't deliver."

Incidentally, during this disastrous tournament, lights were installed in the Stadium for three nights, but attendance was very poor despite perfect weather. It is inconceivable that this could happen today.

In the twenties Gatcomb proposed that the Stadium be named after Louis Carruthers, president of the West Side when the Stadium was built. "He arranged for the complicated trading of real estate parcels and the new layout of the street that made the Stadium possible. But they voted the proposal down, probably because it would have hurt Mike [Julian] Myrick's feelings."

Myrick had much to do with negotiating a ten-year contract with the USLTA that made the Stadium feasible. One of the few members who opposed the Stadium project said that the ten-year contract guaranteeing a major annual event to the club was just a piece of paper, Gatcomb recalls. Like a good stock certificate, it was a piece of paper of considerable value.

Gatcomb has stored in his mind things that do not turn up in written accounts of club history. For instance, insufficient subscriptions to Stadium seats created a capital shortfall that required the club to liquidate securities it held and to take out a mortgage that was not paid off until 1950. When tournament revenues proved inadequate, the club borrowed money from the USLTA. This debt was wiped out in 1943.

Such details are of little public interest, but they help to breathe life into the dull substance of real estate. And real estate is what Forest Hills is all about. It began as a residential real estate development. The current resistance of the neighborhood to putting lights in the Stadium comes from residents who like their streets quiet at night, not filled with tennis spectators.

Gatcomb says that the Forest Hills Gardens Corporation has the right to veto the holding of non-sports events at the club, and did disapprove a proposed light opera series years ago. But the club is the corporation's largest member. The corporation did not keep the Beatles out!

The West Side spirit can be summed up by the word continuity. There seems to be a determination that the club continue along traditional lines, but lines that can be adjusted to changing circumstances. Hence the installation of clay courts—and hence the continuing dissatisfaction among some members about the loss of many grass courts, an adjustment that goes too far for them. The loss of TV revenue to the USLTA also outrages some of these same members. The factional tensions in recent months have been so severe as to arouse fears that the club may be tearing itself apart.

Significantly, the quarreling generally occurs during the winter. Once spring comes and the members are out on the courts, the purpose of the club again is clarified. It exists for tennis matches and not for shouting matches.

Reflecting this fundamental fact is a full page in the club membership booklet of its active members ranked by the USLTA and the Eastern Lawn Tennis Association:

USLTA Rankings, 1973
men's singles, Vitas Gerulaitis, no. 21
men's doubles, Vitas Gerulaitis, no. 10
men's 60 singles, Edward L. Dame, no. 18
men's 60 doubles, Edward L. Dame, no. 7
men's 70 singles, Clarence C. Chaffee, no. 1
men's 70 doubles, Clarence C. Chaffee, no. 1

ELTA Rankings, 1973
men's singles, Vitas Gerulaitis, no. 3
men's doubles, Vitas Gerulaitis, no. 1
women's singles, Ruta Gerulaitis, no. 9
boys' 16 singles, Jonathan Gross, no. 3
boys' 14 singles, Raymond Disco, no. 14
girls' 18 singles
   Ruta Gerulaitis, no. 5
   Laurey Gross, no. 3
   Julia Zukas, no. 23
girls' 16 singles, Laurey Gross, no. 12
senior men's singles, Tony DeGray, no. 25
senior men's doubles, Tony DeGray, no. 7
senior men's 60 singles, Edward L. Dame, no. 2
senior women's doubles, Louise Cilla-Carmen Boland, no. 1

25

FOREST HILLS OBSERVED

For anyone who has not been to Forest Hills during the middle of a national tournament it is hard to imagine just how much is going on at the same time. The Open is really a festival of tennis, with as many as sixty-four matches being played in one day. No report, no telecast, can capture the sensation of plentitude and spectacle involving well over 1,000 men and women, including players, umpires, ball boys, committee officials, the press and the scores of working people employed to hold the whole thing together.

An Australian tennis pro coming to the Open for the first time in 1974 called it "electrifying." No other American tennis event attracts 300 members of the press, for example. Forest Hills evidently needs this big a press corps to get the many stories out, the pictures taken, the broadcasts made.

One of the benefits of moving the nationals to Forest Hills in 1915 was the instant recognition the event gained from a much bigger press attendance than traveled to Newport. Newspapers, national magazines and then radio and newsreel, all with headquarters in Manhattan, eagerly covered the big matches. The West Side has always had an incomparable advantage over any other club by being in the news capital of the world.

Of all the reporters who covered Forest Hills, Allison Danzig, now retired from *The New York Times*, stands out. His style of reporting is no longer fashionable, but it is still a pleasure to read. Here are two sentences from his account of Lacoste's defeat of Tilden in the finals of 1927:

> Tilden in the years of his most ruthless sway, was never a more majestic figure, never played more upon the heart-strings of a gallery than he did yesterday as he gave the last ounce of his superb physique to break through a defense that was as enduring as rock, and failed; failed in spite of the fact that he was three times at set point in the first chapter, in spite of the fact that he led at 3–1 in the second set, and once again in spite of the fact that he held the commanding lead of 5–2 in the third set and was twice within a stroke of taking this chapter.
>
> He failed because youth stood in the balance against him—youth in the person of an untiring sphinx that was as deadly as fate in the uncanny perfection of his control, who assimilated the giant Tilden's most murderous swipes and cannonball serves as though they were mere pat balls and who made such incredible saves as to have broken the spirit of nine men out of ten.

Danzig has happily preserved some of his best stories in *The Fireside Book of Tennis* (1972), which he edited with Peter Schwed, along with those of other writers in the past like Al Laney of the New York *Herald Tribune,* John R. Tunis, Arthur Daley, Paul Gallico, John Kieran and Bob Considine.

Not available, alas, are the radio broadcasts of NBC's Ted Husing, whose hushed intonations set the style for the electronic media. Radio, which began carrying tennis in 1921 when KDKA of Pittsburgh reported matches between Australian and British teams at the Allegheny Country Club, made Forest Hills come alive from coast to coast. At the same time newsreels invariably showed one shot of people in the Stadium turning their heads back and forth.

TV came in during the Kramer–Gonzales era, and the first colorcast was made at Forest Hills during the 1955 Davis Cup matches with Australia. In the sixties Bud Collins, who had been covering tennis for the Boston *Herald* and coaching the game at Brandeis University, brought a new touch to telecasting, a genial lightness of tone combined with an encyclopedic knowledge of the game. Only Bud Collins, now a columnist for the Boston *Globe,* could get away with describing the sky over Wimbledon as a varicose blue. His Public Broadcasting System coverage has brought hundreds of hours of intelligently reported tennis to the aficionados.

Viewers today are the beneficiaries of an expertise unavailable in the days of radio. As commentators, former stars can put you inside the minds of the players and heighten the tension by pointing out the significance of a particular moment. "He *has* to get his first serve in. His second serve gets powdered every time. This puts enormous pressure on him." And so on.

Since the Open, media coverage of tennis has increased geometrically.

215

The New York Times now has three reporters who cover tennis, Neil Amdur, Parton Keese and Charles Friedman, and Dave Anderson does occasional columns on the sport. *World Tennis* is now a monthly with a circulation of 150,000; it started in 1953 as a newsletter. *Tennis U.S.A.*, the USLTA magazine, is sent monthly to all members. A third monthly, *Tennis*, claiming the largest circulation of any tennis magazine, is owned by the New York Times Company and is the official publication of the United States Professional Tennis Association.

To handle the press the West Side has had its member George McGann, who heads the Australian Consolidated News Service, run a volunteer press committee coordinated with the USLTA's own public relations department. Since there are only seventy places in the press box under the marquee, it is necessary to limit them to those filing daily reports. Twice this number of writers, editors, photographers and public relations people get so-called B passes and tickets to the Stadium as well as the right to enter the clubhouse area.

All these media people, therefore, have access to the players between matches, and many interviews are conducted in the locker rooms. Attempts to bar the press from the locker rooms have failed, and players have learned to say no when they don't want to be bothered by reporters.

"I don't need you guys," a player told a photographer of some importance. "I make my own image by winning."

"Unless we report it, kid, no one will ever know," was the reply. And that's why a player, immediately after a match, will dutifully follow an official to a tent to be interviewed in sweaty clothes. Deadlines demand an immediate quote. After the finals there are more than a hundred newsmen at the players' press conference.

The umpires make up another corps of 250 at Forest Hills. They wear blue blazers with USLTA insignias and they come from as far off as Texas —businessmen, housewives, teaching tennis pros, almost all tennis players themselves who have brought their gear to play a few sets of doubles before the matches. They used to work for the honor of it, but since the players get paid, the umpires want something too.

In 1974 the USLTA set aside $6,000 for umpiring costs. The umpires get $6 a day plus a meal and two tickets and a drink. James W. Sullivan, chairman of the New England umpires, who started umpiring at Longwood in 1947, explained in an interview that it cost him $250 out of pocket to come to Forest Hills.

The umpires work two to five matches a day, either in the chair or on a line under the direction of chief umpire Jack Stahr. As players are eliminated, the number of umpires available declines, even though there is work for them in the Pepsi-Cola juniors or mixed-doubles events. Taking lip from players and their coaches is not pleasant, and umpires form strong and adverse opinions about players who remonstrate frequently. For the

Comedian Alan King takes his tennis very seriously. Of the Open he says: "It took tennis from the class and gave it to the mass."

George McGann, chairman of the West Side's press liaison committee, hosts an annual press tournament with the help of Dagny Woodcock, wife of the club pro.

219

With 34 million Americans playing tennis, the equipment industry has boomed. The mere appearance of a racket at Forest Hills is no longer as promotionally valuable as it once was. Rod Laver endorses the products of twenty-nine companies.

*David Levine,
the Daumier of
American cartoonists,
is an avid tennis player.
Here is his impression of
some of the players
at Forest Hills.*

Jimmy Connors   *Arthur Ashe*

ump the good player is the player who accepts all calls with patient understanding.

"Do you make bad calls?" an umpire from Texas was asked.

"Certainly."

"Do you reverse yourself?"

"Never."

Umpires sometimes steal the show. Hank Quinn, a teaching tennis pro
from Elbow Beach, Bermuda, wears a handsome coconut straw hat with a
large brush sticking up from the band. In an early-round Stadium match
that Nastase was winning easily in 1974, the Rumanian grew bored with
the game and danced over to Quinn and snatched the hat and put it on
for a moment.

The Open requires ninety-five ball boys and girls. Bill Talbert was a
ball boy until he was twenty-one. Stan Smith once failed to qualify as a
ball boy in California because he was too clumsy at the time. Candidates
are tested for their speed of foot and ability to throw the ball, and girls
are equally acceptable now.

Michel Golden, a sixteen-year-old ball girl, comes to Forest Hills for
the money and for the exposure to the players. She gets $2 an hour, and

Billie Jean King   *Evonne Goolagong*   *Vitas Gerulaitis*

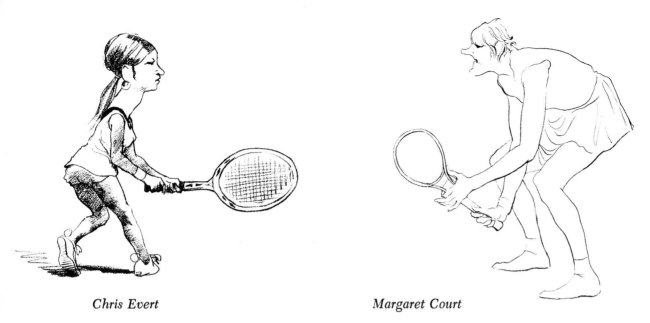

Chris Evert

Margaret Court

if she stays the whole tournament she can earn $120. In the morning before the matches she shows up with a racket, looking for a game with anyone. She is one of those juniors with aspirations to be ranked, and she spends the summer playing tournaments, spending four or five hours a day on the courts. There were no ball girls before the sixties, and they used to work for nothing before the seventies.

A match may take only an hour, sometimes two, but not three any longer. What to do the rest of the day if you are a player—or a member with a ticket, for that matter? No one can watch tennis all day long. So there is a great deal of strolling, glancing at matches for a moment, chatting, munching hot dogs (which are always overpriced, according to the press) and, for those with passes, hanging around the clubhouse terrace.

Here an outdoor-café atmosphere prevails. People at the tables eat lunch, sip cocktails. Others hang around the two outdoor bars. The drinking is not heavy. Some of the players will drink beer. But the favorite quencher is called a Bermuda, a tall iced drink made up of equal parts of ginger ale, sweetened orange and lemon juice, with a slice of lime. It costs 75 cents, and each drink is individually made. No one seems to know its origin, and it appears to be unique to the West Side Tennis Club.

Ilie Nastase

Stan Smith

Pancho Gonzales

There is a bar in the men's locker room where the great players congregate, with or without towels around their middles, after showering. Unlike the locker room of Madison Square Garden or Shea Stadium, it is not a players' preserve. It is a club locker room that the players are allowed to use. Someday there may be locker rooms built under the Stadium, but until then players rub elbows with members, umpires and newsmen, and share their problems sometimes with anyone who will listen.

There is an attic locker room, which on hot days becomes a real cooker, a hell of a place for a player to come to in the middle of a long match to change and try to cool off. But it is all part of Forest Hills. In a small lounge there is color TV to watch, magazines to read and always a backgammon game to get into. Millions of dollars' worth of athletes lounge in leather chairs, getting their precious toes stepped on by perfect strangers. For the amusement of anyone who is looking, Ilie Nastase puts his racket on the floor and dances on it to loosen up the strings, then departs for the court with a loop of gut in his hand.

Many people dislike the West Side Tennis Club because it is a club—and therefore exclusive. Many players resent the length of the U.S. Open, which is not as profitable to them as shorter tournaments are. And many spectators groan when one of their favorites double-faults and seems not to be putting everything into a particular match. But if the West Side Tennis Club were to announce tomorrow that it no longer wanted to host the U.S. Open and was selling the Stadium to a developer, there would be sorrow and a genuine sense of loss. One need only remember the outburst of feeling and nostalgia at the passing of the polo grounds and Ebbets Field. Similar to those great sport arenas that are no more, Forest Hills was and is the final testing ground of heroes and, God knows, in every day and age we need our heroes. The place somehow evokes the past in all its glory, while enlivening the present with a feeling of continuity.

There is something reassuring about Forest Hills. Even with clay courts, which are nothing that new—just more numerous—it has the look of an unchanging garden in the middle of concrete barrenness. A sense of enchantment is inescapable. The thousands of fans who love great tennis do not laugh when someone mentions "the magic of Forest Hills." To them it is a real and living thing.

The grass must go.

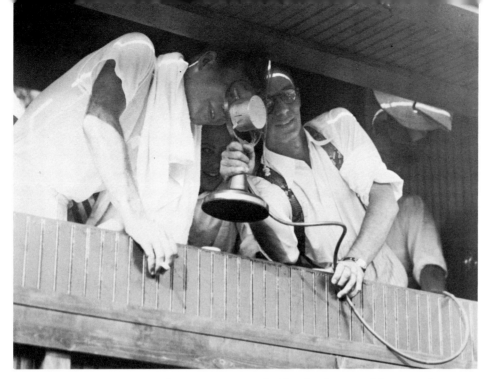

Ted Husing, the great radio sportscaster, holds the heavy old microphone for John Doeg, the 1930 singles champion. From this wooden booth above the Stadium court, Husing described in hushed tones each shot for listeners, who could hear the sounds of the court. Such broadcasts gave Forest Hills a nation-wide fame.

Tournament is a word derived from the old French word *tournier,* to turn around. Jousting cavaliers charging with blunted lances on padded mounts would try to unseat one another in a joust, and then turn around for a second try. Court tennis took over the language of chivalry, and a tournament became an elimination to determine the champion of anything.

The cup presented to the winner is related to the myth of the Holy Grail. Originally a trophy was a monument celebrating a victory in classical times. In medieval mythology the trophy became an end in itself, a talisman of salvation available only to the purest and most enduring knight. Although the myth is Christian in English literature, it is undoubtedly of pre-Christian origin.

Psychologically man seems to need to seek perfection, and his quest has taken many forms. Most of us are spectators of the quest. By our presence we not only witness the contest for the record; we ourselves are in some mysterious way spiritually benefited. Tennis is a game, but a game is a contest, a struggle. Fun and exciting to watch, it is a deadly serious encounter to the players. It means literally everything to them at the time.

It is because Forest Hills has taken tennis so seriously that its annual events have become the tournament of tournaments. Nothing lasts forever, and someday for some reason another place may be preferred as an arena for the culminating tennis matches of the season. But even then Forest Hills will be recalled as that enchanted place where men and women played the game of tennis, struggling with all their physical and spiritual powers for a silver cup, a trophy of triumph and a symbol of one sort of perfection.

223

Bud Collins, of the Boston Globe, one of the game's pioneer telecasters, won the Allison Danzig trophy for tennis reporting in 1968. Allison Danzig, the leading tennis writer for two generations, now retired from The New York Times, *stands in the middle, while Walter Elcock of Brookline, Massachusetts, makes the presentation. In 1974 Elcock was elected president of the International Lawn Tennis Federation.*

BOulevard 8-2300

THE WEST SIDE TENNIS CLUB
Forest Hills, New York 11375

Junior Candidates

 GUEST PASS

*This guest pass will
admit one person into
the U.S. Open Club on*

September 2, 1974

U.S. **10c**

TENNIS
1874·1974

FIRST DAY OF ISSUE

FOREST HILLS N.Y.
AUG
31
1974
11375

Going to Forest Hills?
Have a ball.

**World Tennis Magazine
invites you to a reception honoring
Mr. John Newcombe**

Mr. Newcombe, the defending champion and
all other participants in the 1974 United States
Open will be our invited guests. Please join us.

8:00 PM The Grand Ballroom
Tuesday, September 3, The Roosevelt Hotel
$15 per person.

We've put together a great buffet supper.
There'll be a lot of music and some fancy
door prizes: A weekend for two at the
Boca Raton Hotel & Club. Two spiffy new
Yamaha Composite Rackets.
And, of course, the drinks are on the house.*

*The house would like to thank our co-hosts:
Ballantine's Scotch, Boca Raton Hotel & Club,
Miller High Life, Old Grand Dad, Gilbey's Gin & Vodka,
Coca Cola Bottling Co. of N.Y., Spalding, Yamaha
and Virginia Slims.

RSVP Roosevelt Hotel
Madison Ave. at 45th St., N.Y., N.Y.
USA (800) 221-2690 NYS (800) 522-6449
NYC (212) 683-6620

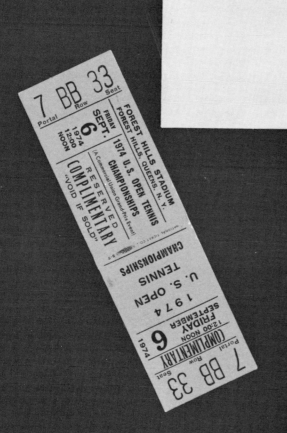

The inscription on the trophy reads:

UNITED STATES
LAWN TENNIS ASSOCIATION
CHALLENGE TROPHY
WOMEN'S SINGLES CHAMPIONSHIP
PRESENTED 1945

227

THE FOREST HILLS ROLL OF CHAMPIONS

MEN'S SINGLES

1915	William M. Johnston	1946	John A. Kramer
1916	R. Norris Williams II	1947	John A. Kramer
1917	R. Lindley Murray	1948	Richard A. Gonzales
1918	R. Lindley Murray	1949	Richard A. Gonzales
1919	William T. Tilden II	1950	Arthur Larsen
1920	William T. Tilden II	1951	Frank Sedgman
1921–23	(Held in Philadelphia)	1952	Frank Sedgman
1924	William T. Tilden II	1953	Tony Trabert
1925	William T. Tilden II	1954	E. Victor Seixas, Jr.
1926	René Lacoste	1955	Tony Trabert
1927	René Lacoste	1956	Kenneth Rosewall
1928	Henri Cochet	1957	Malcolm J. Anderson
1929	William T. Tilden II	1958	Ashley J. Cooper
1930	John H. Doeg	1959	Neale Fraser
1931	H. Ellsworth Vines, Jr.	1960	Neale Fraser
1932	H. Ellsworth Vines, Jr.	1961	Roy Emerson
1933	Frederick J. Perry	1962	Rodney Laver
1934	Frederick J. Perry	1963	Rafael Osuna
1935	Wilmer L. Allison, Jr.	1964	Roy Emerson
1936	Frederick J. Perry	1965	Manuel Santana
1937	J. Donald Budge	1966	Frederick Stolle
1938	J. Donald Budge	1967	John Newcombe
1939	Robert L. Riggs	1968	Arthur Ashe
1940	Donald McNeill	1969	Rodney Laver
1941	Robert L. Riggs	1970	Kenneth Rosewall
1942	Frederick R. Schroeder, Jr.	1971	Stan Smith
1943	Joseph R. Hunt	1972	Ilie Nastase
1944	Frank A. Parker	1973	John Newcombe
1945	Frank A. Parker	1974	James Connors

WOMEN'S SINGLES

1921	Molla Bjurstedt Mallory	1948	Margaret Osborne du Pont
1922	Molla Bjurstedt Mallory	1949	Margaret Osborne du Pont
1923	Helen Wills	1950	Margaret Osborne du Pont
1924	Helen Wills	1951	Maureen Connolly
1925	Helen Wills	1952	Maureen Connolly
1926	Molla Bjurstedt Mallory	1953	Maureen Connolly
1927	Helen Wills	1954	Doris Hart
1928	Helen Wills	1955	Doris Hart
1929	Helen Wills	1956	Shirley J. Fry
1930	Betty Nuthall	1957	Althea Gibson
1931	Helen Wills Moody	1958	Althea Gibson
1932	Helen H. Jacobs	1959	Maria E. Bueno
1933	Helen H. Jacobs	1960	Darlene R. Hard
1934	Helen H. Jacobs	1961	Darlene R. Hard
1935	Helen H. Jacobs	1962	Margaret Smith
1936	Alice Marble	1963	Maria E. Bueno
1937	Anita Lizana	1964	Maria E. Bueno
1938	Alice Marble	1965	Margaret Smith
1939	Alice Marble	1966	Maria E. Bueno
1940	Alice Marble	1967	Billie Jean Moffitt King
1941	Sarah Palfrey Cooke	1968	Virginia Wade
1942	Pauline Betz	1969	Margaret Smith Court
1943	Pauline Betz	1970	Margaret Smith Court
1944	Pauline Betz	1971	Billie Jean Moffitt King
1945	Sarah Palfrey Cooke	1972	Billie Jean Moffitt King
1946	Pauline Betz	1973	Margaret Smith Court
1947	Louise Brough	1974	Billie Jean Moffitt King

INDEX

Page numbers in italics refer to illustrations.

233

236

238

239

West Side Tennis Club (*cont.*)
210-11; women in, 31, 105; and writing by tennis players, 121
White, Stanford, 30, 62
Whitepot, Long Island, 44, 45
Whitman, Malcolm, 35, *57*, 63, 132
Whitman, Walt, 17
Whitney, Caspar, 30
Wiesbaden, clay from, 141
Wightman, George, 99
Wightman, Hazel Hotchkiss, 99, 104, 109, *110*, 113-14, 132, 134, 138
Wightman Cup, 109, 227
Wightman Cup matches, 17, 109, 113, *128*, 138; 1949 team, *174*
Wilding, Anthony, 55, 56, 57, *58*
Williams, Owen, 200
Williams, Richard Norris, 52, 55, 56, *58*, 59, 65, 69, 72, *82*, 85, 86, 90, 94, 107, *111*, 115, 119, 124; and Johnston, 74, 78, 79, 94, 95
Wills, Helen, later Moody, 80, 99, 103, 104, *105*, 109, 113-14, 115, 122, 136, *137*, 141, 149, 171, 183; character and temperament, 114, 133-34; and Jacobs, 98, *110*, 134-35, *138*; and Lenglen, 102; and McKane, 113, 114; and Mallory, 114
Wilson, Woodrow, 64, 87
Wimbledon, 17, 18, 29, 35, 55, 59, 63, 85, 86, 99, 101, 109, *112*, *114*, 121, 123, 132, 134, 135, 141, 142, 147, 148, 149, 151, 164, 168, 172, 176, 181, 196, 209; boycotted, 32, 193; clothes of players, 136, 138; grass courts, 21, 198-99; and open tennis, 187, 191; professional tournament, first, 191; stadium, 105; subsidized, 201; tie breakers,

201; Tilden named as world champion, 91, 93-94
Wingfield, Major Walter Clopton, 28
Wolfmann, Ernie, 16
Women as tennis players, 22, 98, 105, 109; clothes, 98, 99, 135-36, 138, 210-11; modern, 183, 209; professionals, 196; in U.S. Open, 209
Women's national championships, 70, 76, 80, 90, 107, 149, 183; at Forest Hills, first, 98, 100, 102; Mallory's record, 103; Wills and Jacobs, 1933, 134-35
Wood, Sidney, *95*, 108, *112*, 136, 139, 143, 148
Woodcock, Dagny, *219*
Woonsocket, R.I., 33
World champion, title given at Wimbledon, 91, 93-94
World Championship Tennis, 182, 192
World Team Tennis, 23, 25, 108, 183, 192, 193
World Tennis, 24, 193, 196, 203, 209, *216*
World War I, 54, 56, 59, 60, 73, 76, 77, 80-81; tennis players in armed forces, 76, 78-79, 82, 85
World War II, 132, 155, 159, 211
Wrenn, Robert D., 71, 72, *82*, 85
Wright, Beals C., 87, 132
Wright & Ditson, 33, *38*, 78

YMCA, 85

Zinderstein, Marion, 104
Zukas, Julia, 213

240

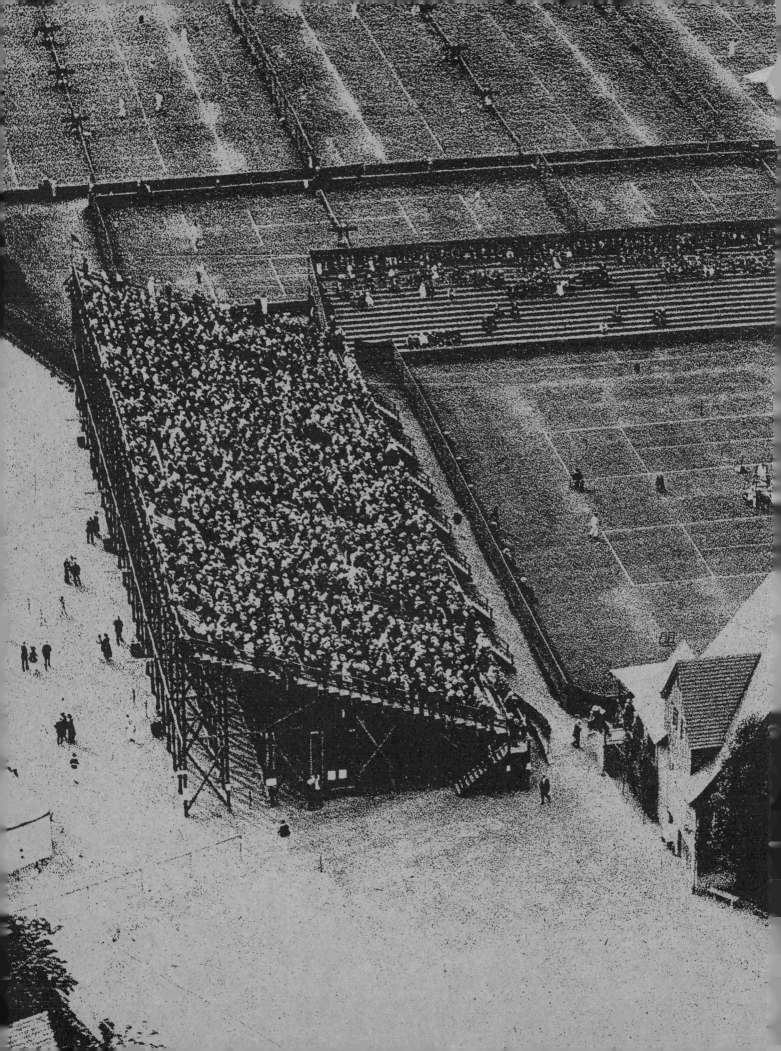